SEAN OLIVER

A Servant's Tray

Cover by

MessengerBoi Communications

Table of Contents

Endorsements

"Belief always determines behavior! In every letter Paul wrote, there is always a list of imperatives that are presented for believers to practice. The practice becomes the evidence and the fruit of faith of the believer's confidence in Jesus. Sean has done an excellent job of following Pauls' pattern of providing practical imperatives and wisdom to assist and encourage believers to provide evidence and fruit of faith as they practice God's word in every aspect of daily life."
– **Dr. Terrance O'Neil** *(Pastor/Teacher)*

"I have had the privilege of watching and knowing Sean as one of his pastors. He writes from the authenticity of a life that has been totally changed by Christ. A Servant's Tray is the more than the insight to a changed life. It is a solid piece of theological work. The gospel, forgiveness, redemption, sanctification, security, identity in Christ is spread through the pages. True freedom from Christ is clearly offered as Sean shares the Biblical truth he has learned and experienced. I can wholeheartedly recommend A Servant's Tray to any one regardless of where they are in their journey of faith."
– **Dennis Henderson** *(National Director of the 6:4 Fellowship)*

"Sean Oliver is no stranger to adversity and those trials have brought him closer to God. In his first book, A Servant's Tray, Sean shares many Bible verses that have helped him navigate and increasingly secular world. Although it is a personal account, the lessons learned will appeal to anyone looking for a fresh prospective on God's Word. He digs deep and you will want to, as well!"
– **Whitney Nelson** *(CEO, Brilliant People, LLC)*

Dedication

I dedicate this book first and foremost to those who gave me mercy and love when I opposed myself.

To my mother, Carolyn Oliver, who instilled in me the vision and confidence of what manhood and sacrifice is all about; to Orville and Ruth Loomis who took the time to show me God's love; and finally, to my grandfather, Wade Oliver, whose discipline, and love kept life meaningful.

I am grateful for each of these individuals' impact in my life and made myself a promise to make them proud.

Prelude

All my life experiences have prepared me for this very moment. My prayers, dedication, and consecration have ushered me into this work. As a child I grew up being told I would make a difference. Like many, a lack of patience and an aversion to a relationship with God led me down a path of moral and physical destruction. The metamorphosis from having no faith in myself to growing a seed of hope took time. Now, through all spiritual blessings in heavenly places in Christ, my transcendent mission is to equip and edify the body of Christ.

This book was written section by section each night as I listened to what the Holy Spirit spoke to me through the Bible, personal revelation, and reflection on things He has taught me thus far in my walk. My hope is that these words will impact and reach you wherever you are in life. As you read, may your spirit be fed, deliverance take place in your heart, and the everyday application of Biblical truths come alive. My prayer for you is that the hope, wisdom, and anointing you need to overcome in the authority of the Holy Spirit will be actualized as you read.

It is my hope that your focus will not be on what the book can do for you, but rather what the anointing from the Holy Spirit in the words of this book can do for you. If you do know Jesus as your Lord and Savior, may you continue in the rest and joy that God's Word promises to those who keep their minds on Him. If you do not know Jesus through a personal relationship, but only by namesake, learn about the freedom and dynamic personal relationship that Jesus Christ offers.

Do you know how much God loves YOU? There is a grace and power available to raise you up from greed, pride, and shackles that bad decisions have bound you with. I give you not wisdom of this world that is perishable, battered, and divisive; but I give you the word of our King Jesus Christ. I give you the wrecking ball of the Spirit to knock down walls that have hindered, deceived, robbed, and abased you long enough. Man, woman, child, saved, or unsaved, I was sent to loose you with the power, authority, Word and anointing of Jesus Christ.

Though you may have opposed yourself and God either willingly or unwillingly, consciously or unconsciously, nothing separates you from God's love or call. Yours and others' prayers have been heard on high in heaven. Just as God heard the cries of the Israelites in the captivity of Egypt, He raised up and sent a man to be His vessel of deliverance for them.

CAUTION! Do not be blinded by circumstances, credentials, or age. For we are not ignorant of Satan's devices. Many of the world's wisdom view King David and Jesus Christ as mere ordinary men and view we who are in Christ as unremarkable women and men. The world's wisdom once said, "David is small, has no experience, and is the youngest of a family of fighting men." The world's wisdom once said, "Jesus! How could He be the Christ when his parents are of no reputation and his father is who knows?" The wisdom of the world says, "Christians are weak and prejudiced and should be tolerated and ignored." People should never look at the outer appearance alone to judge the worth or purpose of a man/woman. If you sow to the flesh you will reap to the flesh, but if you sow to the Spirit you will reap of the Spirit. God knew what you needed at such a time as this. As you read each page

allow yourself to be served words of life.

Introduction

The words in the pages of this book were written to

demonstrate how God's Word is applicable in

everyday circumstances. The scriptures in the pages

of this book will allow you to see how individuals in

times past have had divine help in navigating trauma,

relationship problems, and decision making that

solved problems in both cities and nations.

Chapter 1
Shackles of Jacob

As the years pass by, certain events take place that will be significant to either our demise or success in life. Such is the case in the life of Jacob, the son of Isaac. Our value is not as simple as weighing achievements in life based upon society's or the world's standards. When we look at our losses and failures in comparison with others who have achieved success by the world's standards, we miss the value of our uniqueness. We must look deeper into ourselves. We must look beyond the size of our bank accounts, the number of friends we have, and our degree of education. We are faced with the expectations we have set for ourselves.

Some of us were manipulated by Satan to believe a lie. Some of us were tempted by the accolades of friends or peers that pressured us into becoming other people's ideas of who we should be. Some of us were even so selfish that we based our lives solely on what we wanted when we wanted it if nobody got hurt. We have all faced circumstances or choices like these before. You are not alone.

Do you think Thomas Edison knew as a child ridiculed for his ideas that he would eventually create life-changing inventions? Do you think that young King David of the Bible, knew that his battles against lions and bears in the outskirts of the countryside were going to be pivotal in his growth as a man of faith? No, neither of these men did!

So let us look at how the decisions, experiences, and heroes we have accepted, believed in, and been captivated by drew us into a web of dreams and expectations that now leave us angry about our career choices, emotionally depleted by broken relationships, and confused about a God who loves us but sometimes seems against us.

How many times did we watch TV and think we wanted to fly like that superhero or look like that fashion model? How many times have we read a hashtag or seen a YouTube video based on an idea we had but never followed through with? Many of the thoughts we entertained or accepted were not ours at all, but Satan's.

We can be all we can be, but the only way to be truly happy is to be all God called us to be. We were created for more than what we have experienced. We have seen parts of that "more" in dreams, thoughts, and perhaps New Years' resolutions, but have not followed through with them.

There once lived someone just like us named Jacob who as a boy, aspired to greatness. Before Jacob was born it was promised he would be a nation, and his eldest brother would serve him.

"And Isaac entreated the Lord for his wife because she was barren: and the Lord was entreated of him, and Rebecca his wife conceived. And the children struggled together within her; and she said, 'If it be so, why am I thus?' And she went to inquire of the Lord. And the Lord said unto her, 'Two nations are in thy womb, and two manner of people shall be separated from thy bowels; and the one people shall

be stronger than the other people; and the elder shall serve the younger." (Genesis 25:21-23)

The scriptures go on to say that as these boys grew, the older brother Esau became a cunning hunter. These scriptures as paraphrased by Sean would read:

Jacob: Mama, when I grow up, I'm going to be a great man. I'll take care of you and make dad proud.

Rebecca: Jacob, I believe you. Therefore, you must always watch and listen. You can learn a lot by just keeping your mouth closed and ears open.

Jacob: I do watch and listen mamma, but daddy only

seems to pay attention to Esau. If he would give me more chances to speak to him...I'd show him what I know. Esau isn't all that smart. I know how to get him to do just what I want; just like you do daddy.

Rebecca: Shhh, Jacob! When you know how to get what you want from people, you don't let them know you do.

Jacob: Why not?

Rebecca: Never tell a person everything you know because then they will know what they know <u>and</u> what you know which means they know more than you.

Jacob: I'll remember mama.

Esau became a man's man. He looked the part of a ragged yet cunning soldier. He was the type of man others tend to follow. When Esau entered a town, heads turned, and bodies just seemed to gravitate towards him hoping just for a moment of his attention. Jacob, on the other hand, was a plain man who mostly stayed home. He was soft spoken and keenly observant, but seldom noticed by others. Esau caused heads to turn while Jacob blended in and always seemed too just be around.

The scriptures say the boys' father loved Esau because he ate the food he hunted. However, Rebecca loved Jacob. Following this narrative, we see a mama's boy in Jacob who was favored by her, always near to her, and told how God had said wonderful things about him to her. Even though Esau was the father's favorite, Jacob was to rule and have the best of his father's legacy.

I was told as a child I could be anything I wanted. Were you ever told this? With such affirmation, how could we not believe we would grow up to be what we chose to be? I always knew from as early as second grade that I would be a lawyer. I thought this, accepted it, and believed nothing could stop me. I had encouragement, a high level of self-esteem, and family approval. But, oh, as the years passed by and I experienced the worldliness of this life, when it came time to be who I envisioned myself to be my web of dreams and plans turned into the shackles of Jacob. The self-confidence string of my web turned into a shackle of fear. The strong will and iron fortitude strings of my web turned into shackles of blinding, unfeeling, unloving, selfish ambition.

When we find ourselves encumbered by the fruits of our disillusionment, we start to ask ourselves what happened. How did I get in this bed again? How did I end up in this cell? How did I get to this low point in my life when the only thing I've done is to try to make everyone I care about happy? The same thing happened to Jacob.

"And Jacob sod pottage: and Esau came from the field, and he was faint: and Esau said to Jacob, 'Feed me, I pray thee, with that same red pottage; for I am faint': therefore, was his name called Edom. And Jacob said, 'Sell me this day thy birthright.' And Esau said, 'Behold I am at the point of dying: and what profit shall this birthright do to me?' And Jacob said, 'swear

to me this day' and he swore unto him: and he sold his

birthright unto Jacob". (Genesis 25:29-33)

By definition, a shackle can be referred to as a metal loop or link closed by a bolt or the act of connecting chains. In Jacob's situation shackles can refer to spiritual loops or links closed by choices, decisions, or depraved perspectives to connect to life's experiences.

To the shackled believer or sinner, never believe the shackles that you allowed to remain won't tighten and eventually strangle you. They leave us a shallow shell of unfulfilled potential and seemingly hopeless potential. Jacob thought the shackles of his past were based on location and circumstances, but he soon found out otherwise. All of us have or will discover at some point that shackles are personal and run as deep as the thoughts that brought them to life.

Jacob fled Esau because of fear and shackles of recompense. We reap what we sow. We are affected by what we hide even when no one else knows what we have hidden. Why and what are you fleeing from, and shackled with? Jacob, fled to a relative's home to seek safety and new aspirations, but never realized that shackles only grow longer and stronger through years of denial. Delayed doesn't mean denied and there's a day of judgment for all the choices we have made. You can look new and start new but if you never deal with the shackles of the past through Christ, then they remain. They may feel lighter on you some days, but shackles always outweigh your joy and twist tighter around new dreams.

"And Laban had two daughters: the name of the elder was Leah and the name of the younger was Rachel. Leah was tender eyed; but Rachel was

beautiful and well favored. And Jacob loved Rachel, and said, 'I will serve thee seven years for Rachel thy younger daughter. '" (Genesis 29:16-18)

"And Jacob served seven years for Rachel; and they seemed unto him but a few days, for the love he had for her. And Laban gathered together all the men of the place, and made a feast. And it came to pass in the evening that he took Leah his daughter and brought her to him: and he went in unto her. And it came to pass, that in the morning, behold, it was Leah: and he said to Laban, 'What is this thou hast done unto me? Did not I serve with thee for Rachel? Wherefore then hast thou beguiled me.?" (Genesis 29:20-23, 25)

Wouldn't you be upset if you were Jacob? We must see that a shackle is never-ending, cruel, and deadly until it is broken. Satan spins a web of deceit, mirages, and false hopes based on evil intents of the heart and unfulfilled potentials. It is what can keep us chained to a past of shackles. Are you weary of changing jobs, friends, churches, or whatever? Are you looking for freedom from your vices? Vices created and shackles un-dealt with: When the dream, plan, or promise created outside of God comes to fruition, we find that the invisible web of deception that once drove you changed into a real live shackle of whatever emotion, loss, or circumstance Satan had planned from the inception of his diabolical scheme. Oh, man or woman of God and/or man or woman of shackled past and present, be not deceived any longer!

"I beseech you therefore, brethren, by the mercies of God, that ye present your bodies a living

sacrifice, holy, acceptable unto God, which is your reasonable service." (Romans 12:1)

The dreams we had that we were just like Michael Jordan or Larry Bird and would play in the N.B.A. were real to us. Even as this dream deteriorated due to drug use, illnesses, and lack of dedication, we still believed. The realization that no matter how many dunks or jump shots we put down, we would never make it without opportunity or a certain degree of talent at a young age began to tighten around our minds. Now we are adults shackled with unfulfilled dreams and memories of past glory and teenage fantasies.

Regardless of what our dashed dreams are, what does it make us? Do we become people that plan, work, and create cutting-edge ideas for the future, but that never possess the dedication or fortitude to bring those plans to pass? Do the shackles of possessiveness create a set of shackles for your family? Or yet are you a Christian who found yourself wanting the anointing of Elijah to be able to work miracles like Jesus or have the impact of a T.D. Jakes or D.L. Moody when speaking only to realize that after years of trying to work at being a Christian something was wrong. Not being led by the Spirit, lukewarm service to the Lord in areas of your life, always desiring the material over the spiritual, and not consecrating or dedicating your whole life to Christ; you needed to re-dedicate, not just self-motivate, to God. Realizing that just to continue with your sanity—in Christ was a miracle? Command those shackles of Satan to set you free in Jesus' name and pause to read Isaiah 10:27, believe, and meditate on it. To the unsaved individual I say, repent, accept Christ as your Lord and Savior, and allow the Holy Spirit to lead you into the paths of righteousness.

Now take a moment to read 1 John 1:1-10 in the Bible. To the saved person, I share this passage from 1 Corinthians 6:11, *"And such were some of you: but ye are washed, but ye are sanctified, but ye are justified in the name of the Lord Jesus, and by the Spirit of our God."*

No matter whether you feel like you are all these things or not, God said you became all these things and much more upon your acceptance of salvation. In the beginning of time God said, "Let there be light," and there was light. He is unchanging and can be trusted.

God says in 2 Corinthians 5:17 that if we are in Christ, we are a new creation. We must look beyond the strongholds, and failings, and shackles Satan has hindered us with.

"For godly sorry worketh repentance to salvation not to be repented of, but the sorrow of the world worketh death." (2 Corinthians 7:10)

"And we know that all things work together for good to them that love God, to them who are the called according to his purpose." (Romans 8:28)

Even with all our experience and shackles, we can still allow God to teach us from them, and free us from them right now. I know they are second nature now, but if you trust in the Lord, he will free you (see John 8:36).

Look at the other choice- a life of entanglement and misery with heaviness of heart. Realize that if Satan wasn't concerned about what we could do with God in us then he would not continue to keep us wrapped in shackles—he would kill us. Satan is real.

We didn't get to this place in life by making bad choices alone. Satan's goal is to steal from us, kill us, and destroy everything in our lives, but God has a plan and purpose for our lives.

Christ said, *"Come unto me, all ye that labor and are heavy laden, and I will give you rest. Take my yoke upon you, and learn of me, for I am meek and lowly in heart: and you shall find rest to your souls. For my yoke is easy, and my burden is light."* (Matthew 11:28-30)

Begin to be led by the Spirit. This is as simple as asking God to help you know and follow the impressions of His Holy Spirit in Jesus' Name. God helps us mature to see these truths. Shackles have hurt, haunted, and in some cases almost killed us. God's yoke can cause us to love and enjoy a day of thoughtful reflection or a night of peaceful sleep. When the power of God is stirred up in you or is drawing you close, it will change not only your life but the lives of those around you.

Jacob realized a change must come and fought for it. *"And Jacob was left alone; and there wrestled a man with him until the breaking of day. And he said, thy name shall be called no more Jacob, but Israel: for as a prince hast thou power with God and with men, and hast prevailed."* (Genesis 32:24-28)

Will you wrestle with God for your freedom, peace, rest, and deliverance? Will you wrestle with God for your life? I know there has been pain and disappointments, but realize as Job did in Job 23:8-10, "Behold I go forward, but he is not there; and backward, but I cannot perceive him: on the left hand, where he doth work, but I cannot behold him: he hideth himself on the right hand, that I cannot see him: but he knoweth the way that I take: when he hath tried me, I shall come forth as gold."

We have been tried, *"Oh taste and see that the Lord is good: Blessed is man that trusteth in him."* (Psalm 34:8)

Let the shackles of Jacob go. You have carried them long enough.

- How can a man hear unless he has life?
- How can a man have life except he has salvation?
- How can a man have salvation lest he be drawn and chosen?
- How can a man that's drawn and chosen to want to be delivered?
- How can a man be delivered but the shackles be broken?
- How can the shackles be broken but the Word go forth?
- How can we have the Word and believe yet not be set free?

And being free mighty man or woman, walk, walk, walk! Walk till you run, run till you fly, fly till you reach heaven, but never forget the anointing broke the shackles off Jacob. Never forget lest the shackles return.

To walk in the freedom of Christ is a glorious, blessed thing, but we must know that the paths and scars the shackles leave are deep and they will take time to heal and mature from. Yes, we have freedom in Christ, yes, we have life and more abundantly, but just as our shackles leave their marks on our skin, they also leave marks on others. There are shackles in every individual's life that surpass gender, color, and tax brackets. The shackle is Satan in the form of evil and the reality of death. This day realize that both were conquered by Jesus Christ's death, burial, resurrection, and ascension.

Can't you hear it? Shhhhh!!!! Listen. Don't think-listen. The trumpet is blowing and the keys to your shackles have been revealed. Would you remain though freedom calls and awaits you? Would you? God meets you where you are. The explanation of your plight, the reidentification of your way to freedom, and the call to rest have been given. No longer be entangled amongst the worries of past, present, and future. Be free, be free, be free! The power of Jacob's shackles is not in the circumstances but in the holding fast to the materials the shackles are made from. By now you know that any shackle is only as strong as the things it is made of. We may not have planned it, but we brought the shackles into existence and with God's help, we can take them out. The choice is ours.

Chapter 2

The Walls You Can't See

Proverbs 29:18 says, "Where there is no vision the people perish,"

The following is an excerpt from the story of blind Bartimaeus. *"Jesus, thou Son of David, have mercy on me," and many charged Bartimaeus that he should hold his peace: but he cried the more a great* deal, *"Thou Son of David, have mercy on me,"* (Mark 10:47-48).

The passage is symbolic of the fact that though we all go through sin or figurative blindness in our lives regardless of the degree or circumstances, but there is hope and freedom found in Jesus Christ *if* we only cry out for His help to see. The Bible says we all have gone astray, and we have built up walls of confused identities or allowed Satan to build up walls of jealousy, pride, fear, insecurity, and more. All these walls were built under disguised thoughts such as "This is what I want," or "I can't help how I am," or "This is what life has made me." These are lies from the enemy, straight from the pits of hell and I rebuke them in Jesus' Name.

You can be who God created you to be and are capable of all things through God who made you and Christ who saved you. You may ask yourself, "How did I reach this point? What led me to arrive at these conclusions? This dark and secluded location in life is not where I want to be." We can't physically see the walls with the naked eye, but we certainly can feel the limited space in which we think and move.

The conversation in this space goes something like this: 'Helllo? Helllloooo? Can anybody hear me? Hey, will somebody answer me? What am I going to do now? I began building this wall to be alone, but now I'm cut off."

When I personally first laid that brick of ignoring people at my discretion, it worked. After a few years I could look a person in the *eye* and not hear a word they said. But as I think about it, maybe not hearing what people said contributed to why I now hear no one when I need someone to speak into my life. I've discovered it to be a wall- a wall of Satan's built up by feelings, emotions, choices, and denials. There are other walls such as complacency, prejudice, joy, and love but these are not what the Holy Spirit is leading me to write about.

I will address:

- Satan's negative walls of tradition, disobedience, and denial
- God's good walls of righteousness, faith, and obedience

It is important to note the distinction between a spiritual wall and spiritual shackle. A spiritual shackle often seems like a restraining detriment limiting us in this life. God may allow shackles to clasp hold of us, but we should never forget what the Lord told Paul, *"My grace is sufficient for thee: for my strength is made perfect in weakness,"* (2 Corinthians 12:9). A wall can be a negative or a positive structure. It can detain and obscure our growth OR stabilize us and others in manifesting God's will and kingdom in this world. The materials that make up the bricks of our walls will dictate whether they are good or evil.

As we proceed, I will be discussing the types of walls that cannot be seen with the naked eye. These unseen spiritual walls are felt in everyone's life around us as well as our own.

Let us look at walls that God speaks of throughout his Word:

- Ephesians 2:14 says, *"For he is our peace, who hath made both one, and hath broken down the middle wall of partition between us."*
- 2 Corinthians 10:3-4 says, *"For though we walk in the flesh, we do not war after the flesh: for the weapons of our warfare are not carnal, but mighty through God to the pulling down of strongholds."*

In both texts, the walls are spiritual. In one text it's called a partition and in the other a stronghold. These days God uses the Holy Spirit, His people, and His Word to assist us in building up walls of His Kingdom. The walls of God can be a spiritual structure that elevates people and gives vision to the lost and faith to the faithless.

Take possession of some mortar of the Holy Spirit. Form bricks of hope, faith, love, and wisdom and allow God to build these walls in and around you to help others and bring you joy. An individual who has Jesus Christ as their cornerstone is one whose walls offer protection for the oppressed and act as a lookout post for the watchmen of God.

The Bible says where sin abounded, grace did much more so. As we build up God's walls, others are building Satan's. The enemy uses enticing things such as carnal thoughts and our flesh (if we allow!!) to build up his kingdom. An individual's walls made up of bricks of envy, pride, etc. are walls or strongholds from which Satan can hinder, oppress, and launch fiery attacks on the people of God. Satan uses walls of division and race to keep people blinded to the life and yoke-breaking power of unity and prayer in Christ.

No matter what point we are at in constructing walls in our lives, there is more work to be done. We can build for God and tear down that which is Satan's.

PART I

A - Walls of Disobedience

Saul was a man who worked in two construction camps. One day he would be the slayer of God's enemies and a valiant king of God's people but the next he was a disobedient, fear-ridden man. Have you witnessed any Sauls in our day? These may be men and women who appear as if they are right in God's will only to have God expose the realities of wanton, reckless disobedience running rampant in their lives.

The power of life and death are in the tongue as illustrated by James 3:10, *"Out of the same mouth proceedeth blessing and cursing."* Through excuses and double-minded thinking, Saul (an anointed man of God) built up walls for God's people, but also walls of Satan that eventually ruined and killed him. We as men and women of God must not become vain or self-righteous in our thinking. Just because we do many things for God, does not mean that we are not also through disobedience to God building up unseen walls of Satan as Saul did. *"Wherefore let him that thinketh he standeth take heed lest he fall."* (1 Corinthians 10:12)

Saul began to build up his wall of disobedience almost from the inception of his anointing as king...

"And Samuel said to Saul, thou hast done foolishly: thou hast not kept the commandment of the Lord thy God, which he commanded thee: for now would the Lord have established thy kingdom upon Israel for ever. But now thy kingdom shall not continue: the Lord has sought him a man after his own heart, and the Lord hath commanded him to be captain over his people, because thou hast not kept that which the Lord commanded there." (1 Samuel 13:13-14)

Saul had just been chosen king and Samuel told him the signs that would verify he was being chosen by God to be king. Samuel also told Saul that after these signs, he should go wait on him at Gilgal for 7 days before he made sacrifices to God. Saul disobeyed using the excuses that people were going to desert him, and he feared the Philistines would attack him before he made prayers God. Though these were partial truths Saul spoke, the bottom line was God gave signs and orders to Saul through Samuel to both verify his kingship and test his obedience. With this first act of disobedience, Saul was on his way to building a wall of separation from God's desires for him.

I hear someone's thoughts now - "That's not fair." The lie, the affair...the one act that can cause division between us and another. Reflect on what it has taken for you to build a wall between yourself and someone else. Sometimes we tell ourselves, "One mistake. God is more loving." Beware, the Word of God says, *"For rebellion is as the sin of witchcraft,"* (1 Samuel 15:23). Whether it is one act or many that has built up your walls, tear them down in the name of Jesus.

Saul's walls, as if not big enough already, steadily grew. *"Wherefore then didst thou do not obey the voice of the Lord, but didst fly upon the spoil, and didst evil in the sight of the Lord?"* (1 Samuel 15:19).

Saul was given orders to destroy the Amalek and all that they had. He disobeyed and allowed the people to keep the animals and chiefest of things. Leaders in the body of Christ must ensure we are not swayed into building up walls of disobedience against God just because others deem them lawful. *"But Peter and John answered and said unto them, 'Whether it be right in the sight of God to hearken unto you more than unto God, judge ye.'"* (Acts 4:19)

Saul's walls of disobedience, loneliness, rage, and rebellion cost him his kingship. If you have a wall of disobedience, begin this moment to ask God to tear it down. He will do it, but you have got to want it and must ask Him! In Jesus' name, I speak a desire of holiness in Christ in you right now.

B - Walls of Carnality

"For to be carnally minded is death." (Romans 8:6)

"So, then they that are in the flesh cannot please God." (Romans 8:8)

The carnal mind (the human natural way of thinking outside of God's will) is another dangerous wall to build. Sometimes this line of thinking can be grounded in good intentions but is totally against God's will and straight up Satan's alley. A good example of this principle in operation is found in the books of Matthew and Luke.

"From that time forth began Jesus to show unto his disciples, how that he must go unto Jerusalem, and suffer many things of the elders and chief priests and scribes, and be killed, and be raised again the third day. Then Peter took him, and began to rebuke him,

saying, be it far from thee, Lord: this shall not be unto thee. But he turned and said unto Peter. Get thee behind me, Satan: thou art an offense unto me: for thou savorest not the things that be of God, but those that be of men." (Matthew 16:21-23)

Wow! Can you imagine how Peter must have felt hearing these words? Jesus was one who called evil/evil and good/good. This type of speaking the truth is not as easy as it would seem, something our lives are witnesses to. Just imagine your best friend, teacher, and confidant telling you he must go and die. Peter felt dread at this revelation and wanted to try to save his friend's life. Wouldn't you feel the same if your friend said that to you? Would you feel the same if Jesus spoke these words to you?

People walk in their own finite thoughts instead of being led by the infinite thinking found in Christ. What looks and sounds best may not always be in God's will. Unless we seek God's wisdom in all decisions, we build up a wall of carnality. One might say, "Well that is only one incident of wrong thinking." Stop and realize that a carnal wall is not built by one thought but is the culmination of multiple carnal thoughts.

"And when his disciples James and John saw this, they said, Lord, wilt thou that we command fire to come down from heaven, and consume them, even as Elijah did? But he turned, and rebuked them, and said, Ye know not what manner of spirit ye are of." (Luke 9:54-55)

To give some context for the above passage, Jesus was about to enter a city on his way to Jerusalem but the people there did not want him to come through their town. The disciples James and John spoke out from a thought process that was contrary to why Jesus was even sent to this world. Jesus came to this world to give life, not take it.

When we are not discerning carnal thoughts from godly thoughts, we are playing Russian roulette with our line of thinking. When we are not actively discerning every wrong idea or thought, we accept another brick in the carnal wall we are building. We cannot continue to think and act "carnally." If we do, one day our wall will reach the point of having boxed us in so tight that we will have become someone too contrary to go to. We may even begin to question is there a God. *"And even as they did not like to retain God in their knowledge, God gave them over to a reprobate mind, to do those things which are not convenient."* (Romans 1:28)

The only way to break down or keep from building a wall of carnality is to stand on Galatians 5:16 and apply it, *"This I say..., walk in the Spirit, and ye shall not fulfill the lust of the flesh."* Seek God's face above anything else and desire what He wants for you in every decision, conversation, and thought.

Pray! Father, in Jesus' Name, I pray that you deliver me from the wall of mediocrity and thinking that I have built in my carnal thinking. Help me to see the possible where impossible once stood, discern where I once accepted, and give me vision not only for myself but also for others. Help me to be all things to all men through and in Christ. Help me to win souls for you in Jesus' name.

Emotions can be to the carnal man devices, weapons, and toys for Satan to operate through. He can play, destroy, and build with these emotions not only in our own lives but in the lives of others also.

However, a godly individual's emotions can be a radar to help meet others' needs through prayer and understanding. They can provide a source of empathy from which one can sympathize and relate to others through. We are to be led by the Spirit, not ruled by our emotions. When being led by the Spirit, we live in victory over carnal thinking that opposes God's perfect thinking.

C - Walls of Tradition

"Beware lest any man spoil you through philosophy and vain deceit, after the tradition of men, after the rudiments of the world, and not after Christ." (Colossians 2:8)

Traditions are what family values and the church viewpoints stem from or grow out of. These can be good things in and of themselves yet are not scriptural to build our lives on. None of these alone can get you into to heaven. Consider this fact: the Pharisees and scribes judged, made laws, and even blasphemed based on tradition.

"Why do thy disciples transgress the traditions of the elders? for they wash not their hands when they eat bread. But he answered and said unto them, why do ye also transgress the commandment of God by your tradition?" (Matthew 15:2-3)

Tradition is fine and dandy in terms of family dinners and proper etiquette but when dealing with a loving God and being led by the Holy Spirit, tradition alone will not do. What are we going to say in the Day of Judgment when Jesus asks why we didn't witness to His people? "Oh, I was waiting on the proper timing and circumstances because bringing up in my conversations at the gym, workplace, or club would be uncouth."

What will Jesus say?

I will tell you what He is going to say, "Depart from me, you worker of iniquity—I never knew you."

You may find my example ridiculous, but daily in our local churches there is lukewarm preaching and dry witnessing through the mask of tradition. Members of families are growing up believing they are Christians simply because their other family members have accepted Christ and become Christians. People are going to church services that differ from the ones their families attended and are saying how foolish people sound speaking in tongues and prophesying.

Because of tradition, people have stopped believing God speaks to us. God's Word says He is the same God yesterday, today, and forever. God is too infinite in His ways to be confined to our finite comprehension and depraved imaginations.

It is no wonder why churches across America are dying when elders and deacons stand on tradition. Carnal tradition has made mausoleums out of church buildings. Where Jesus is lifted, he will draw people in. Stop making excuses for buildings that can seat 250 or more and only have a weekly attendance of 80-100 people. The truth is that persecution will not kill the church, but carnal traditions already are.

I remind you through the scriptures this traditional viewpoint is not only not of God but is of the same tactics Satan used on people in Jesus' time. "And when he was come into his own country, he taught them in the synagogue in so much that they were astonished and said, whence hath this man this wisdom, and these mighty works? Is not this a man; whence then hath this man all these things? And they were offended in him. But Jesus said unto them *"A prophet is not without honor, save in his own country, and in his own house."* (Matthew 13:54-67)

Tradition then and now has people believing if they are familiar or unfamiliar with an individual that this matters as to whether God can use them. We as a church must stop saying, "Who? What is his background? Where did he matriculate? How large is his congregation?"

God chose the foolish things and abased people of this world to demonstrate his power to change and use anyone:

"Woe unto you, Scribes, and Pharisees, hypocrites! Because ye build the tombs of the prophets, and garnish the sepulchers of the righteous, and say if we had been in the days of our fathers, we would not have

been partakers with the in the blood of the prophets. Wherefore ye be witness unto yourselves, that ye are the children of them which killed the prophets. Wherefore, behold, I send unto you prophets, and wise men, and scribes: and some of them ye shall kill and crucify; and some of them shall ye scourge in your synagogues, and persecute them from city to city." (Matthew 23:29,31,34)

Stop despising people because they belong to a different denomination. We must stop denying what the Holy Spirit has been saying. These revelations are not just pieces of information for us to reject or receive. They are water to our thirsty souls.

Reader do not look at this scripture in a historical abstract view. We must look at ourselves now! Has the wall of tradition in your life and your church's spirituality silently assassinated God's prophets, wise men, and scribes who live among us? Satan uses no new tricks, just different people.

This is my prayer for you. Right now, in Jesus' name, I pull down the strongholds of carnal traditions hindering any person reading this book. Lord, your Word says our weapons are not carnal but mighty through God to the pulling down of strongholds, casting down imaginations, and everything high thing that exalteth itself against the knowledge of God. I pray for an open mind and heart for God's Word and His people for each reader of these words in Jesus' name.

D - Walls of Denial

"And when they had kindled a fire in the midst of the hall, and were set down together, Peter sat down among them. But a certain maid beheld him as he sat by the fire; end earnestly looked upon him, and said, this man was also with him. And he denied him, saying,

Woman I know him not. And after a little while another

saw him, end said, thou art also of them. And Peter

said, Man, I am not. And about the space of one hour

after another confidently affirmed, saying, of a truth this

fellow also was with him; for he is a Galilean. And Peter

said, Man I know not what thou sayest. And

immediately, while he yet spake the cock crew. And the

Lord turned and looked upon Peter." (Luke 22:55-61)

In Mark, the description of Peter's denial lists the specific areas in which Peter denied Christ: the first was in the palace, the second on the porch, and finally it was nearer to the street that the Bible says Peter denied Christ by cursing and swearing (Mark 14:66-71). Can you see how repeated denials of Christ pushed Peter further from Christ's presence and the awareness of conviction from the Holy Spirit?

When building a wall of denials, we slowly but steadily put-up bricks that can cut us off from hearing

God's correction, guidance, and will. So many Christians today deny a sin problem in areas of their lives that are sensitive and controversial. After repeated denials, the wall is so big that what would have been a normal opportunity to work in their lives to help their children through illness or their boss' bad attitude is gone.

Maybe you have heard someone say, "God is so good and powerful; I believe He can take care of me forever," and then in the next breath say, "The church isn't meeting my needs and I find reading my Bible boring." I know these are extreme examples, but they illustrate how people speak of godliness but disclaim the power of God and prayer in areas that God and prayer are needed. We must stop making excuses and building this blinding wall of denial. We must believe and act knowing God is our answer. Prayer does change things. We must stop making excuses for God to fail us and start building walls such as faith and obedience that God can use to protect His people and work.

Faith without works is dead. Denying God, the opportunity to use and lead us because of the wall of denial is showing God we don't believe His Word. Jesus saw all of Peter's denials but understood. Had not Peter repented of these acts God would have had to deal with this wall of unconfessed sin on judgment day. Let us be like Peter and repent. Tear down the wall of denial and build the walls of God's spiritual kingdom in both Word and deed. Ask God to show you any masked bricks in your life that make up the walls you and Satan have built on. Ask God, in Jesus' name, to mercifully help you tear them down through prayer, fasting, and discernment.

I can see this scenario in my mind where I haven't seen some of these people in so long.

Me: Excuse me. Do you remember me?

Another person: Why wouldn't I? I see you every day. Even though you look right through me and never respond to my hellos I know you.

Me: Ummm, ahhh. I apologize and want you to know I have been wrong in my indifference and treatment of you.

PART II

A - Walls of Righteousness

"And they that shall be of thee shall build the old waste places: thou shalt raise up the foundations of man generations; and thou shalt be called, The repairer of the breach, The restorer of paths to dwell in." (Isaiah 58:12)

The time has come to build up God's Kingdom. As Peter said, *"I have laid the foundation, and another buildeth thereon. But let every man take heed how he buildeth thereupon. For other foundation can no man lay than that is laid, which is Jesus Christ,"* (1 Corinthians 3:10-11).

Anything you or I build must be founded on Jesus Christ and his righteousness, lest it fall. Whether it be business, family, ministry, or self; it must be on and in Christ's name to stand. God is always looking for people to build pieces in His Kingdom. There is no qualification except that we must have accepted Jesus as the Lord and head of our lives.

Maybe you have heard of a great builder of walls of righteousness for the kingdom of heaven: Moses, your local pastor, your brethren in Christ, or even you. One builder of righteous walls stands out amongst them in leadership, planning, and example and that is Nehemiah. He had a hand in rebuilding the walls around Jerusalem. Nehemiah's plan of action and building of walls of righteousness for God are exceptional and could fill a whole book on their own. I want to briefly summarize the ways in which Nehemiah built a specific wall of righteousness around Jerusalem because we can apply those same tactics to achieve growth in our lives and churches:

1. *Take note of the needs of church and self by asking and listening.* (Nehemiah 1:2-3)
2. *Fast, pray, and make requests to God for a way to make a difference and then obey what the Holy Spirit*

through God's Word is saying to you. (Nehemiah 1:4-11)

3. *Ask God for boldness to get what is needed to build and rely on help from fellow Christians.* (Nehemiah 2:4-8, 19-20)

4. *Pray through obstacles.* (Nehemiah 4:1-4)

5. *Be an encourager and reminder of God's faithfulness by sharing your own personal stories and witness with others.* (Nehemiah 4:14)

6. *Make people aware and prepared for situations that may arise concerning doing God's work.* (Nehemiah 4:15-23)

7. *Hear, act, and speak out against wrongs and warn of punishment for wrongs done against God's people.* (Nehemiah 5:1-13)

8. *Be an example and know God is your reward.* (Nehemiah 5:14-19)

9. *Listen to God and do not be moved by circumstances.* (Nehemiah 6:10-14)

The last example of what contributes to a wall of righteousness also entails the fact that God will reveal people and things than would hinder us or seek to place the bricks of unrighteousness in our walls. Proverbs 3:5-6 states plainly that if we trust in and acknowledge God, He will give us understanding and lead us to build a wall of righteousness. Some attributes it takes to build such a wall are perseverance, determination, tenacity, vision, and godly wisdom. God freely gives us all these things in Christ. As we allow the Holy Spirit to work in us, He will build a wall of righteousness. Build a wall, build a wall, and build for our children, for our families, for our God. Build a wall of righteousness, for someone built a wall that saved us.

It is so rewarding interacting with and helping in the things of God. For me personally, not letting the little things get to me has helped a lot. Sometimes I will still get upset with others, but ultimately, I would rather work things out than resurrect old walls and be alone again. Thank you, Lord.

B - Walls of Faith and Obedience

"But without faith it is impossible to please him: For he that cometh to God must believe that he is." (Hebrews 1:6)

Every man or woman who will enter the Kingdom of Heaven must have a wall of faith. I am not going to even speak of the things that faith is not. What I will do is tell you how to build up your walls of faith. First, your faith must be founded in Christ Jesus alone because anything else is unstable and can be demolished by any whim of Satan or question you cannot answer inside yourself. *"Faith cometh by hearing, and hearing by the word of God."* (Romans 10:17)

So many people go to churches, and feast with their eyes and ears and leave as empty as they came. The brick that is vital in building the walls of faith is mixing our hearing and seeing with belief and action. *"Even so faith, if it hath not works is dead, being alone. Yea a man, may say, thou hast faith, and I have works: show me faith without thy works, and I will show thee my faith by my works. Thou believest that there is one God; thou doest well: the devils also believe, and tremble. But wilt thou know, O vain man, that faith without work is dead."* (James 2:17-20)

Works follow faith. If a person has works and no faith, they are dead works in God's sight. If a person has faith, good works will always follow. The brick of works is one we must have in our walls of faith.

A person who has a great wall of faith also has an inner wall of obedience. An example of this is Daniel. When Daniel was told of the signing of a decree that said no man could ask petition of any God or man for thirty days, save of the king only, yet he be cast into the den of lions he went into his house and prayed as usual; out in the open (see Daniel 6:6-10). Daniel did not change one thing to simply please the king, for he was a man of obedience and faith and knew what the king was doing was against God. Daniel had the faith in God to trust Him with his welfare. With strong walls of obedience, a man can face trials, persecutions, and tests without being moved by circumstances.

How many of us would be able to withstand a death threat and be confident and obedient enough to God to know that if we just continued our daily walk without any change, He would save us? I aim daily for this kind of walk, and I know that as my walls of obedience and faith grow, my resilience against fear and Satan's other tactics become stronger. Daily we must strive to obey all laws and people that are not contrary to the Word of God. If we humble ourselves to others for the sake of being obedient to God, we will see the effects of each satanic attack move or change our mood less and less.

Our walls of faith and obedience are not built just to defeat Satan. They are to help others stand firm in Christ. Every wall has a gate. We are to stand at our gate ready to assist our fellow believers and warriors in the war against Satan. We must not stop adding bricks to our walls of righteousness, faith, and obedience and we will continue to see the benefits in ourselves, our family, and in the church. Remember, to stop building or tearing down one wall is to establish or rebuild another. There is no lunch break or vacation. Right now, important work is at hand, but when you get weary know that in eternity is rest.

I am not a fluke, a fake, or a figment of your imagination. I am a man, a mountain of God, a vessel bringing forth the meat and milk of God. Don't look at my race, my education, or the fluency in which I speak. Watch God in me and through me. Realize the words I have written are difference makers, wall breakers, and wall builders not because I said so, but because these words are from the Holy Spirit. They are a wrecking ball of deliverance knocking down walls and punching holes in strongholds that once held you. Foremost, it is God meeting you where you are at. You need to know someone understands where you have been and what you have been through. God sees you and He knows so now the only thing left for you to do is build up unseen walls of God in and around you.

Chapter 3
The Mighty Can't Stand Alone

"And when Moses' father-in-law saw all that, he did to the people, he said, What is this thing that thou doest to the people? Why sittest thou thyself alone, and all the people stand by thee from morning unto even? Thou wilt surely wear away both thou, and this people that is with thee: for this thing is too heavy for thee; thou art not able to perform it thyself alone." (Exodus 18:14,18)

This scripture goes on in Exodus 18:19-22 to tell how Jethro gives Moses' counsel to place rulers over the people and to judge the people at all seasons. Every small matter they shall judge, and every great matter they should bring to Moses. He also told Moses to teach the people God's ordinances and laws and show them how they must walk before God and what work they must do.

These are truths which every mighty individual of God must learn and utilize. Do not think that to be a mighty individual of God you must be of a certain age or gender as King David was mighty at a young age, Prophetess Deborah also, and the prophet Samuel as a child. To be mighty in God's eyes takes righteousness, constant obedience, and a searchable heart.

We often make the mistake of believing that we cannot do works like these individuals God chose. This is a lie from the pits of hell. Many people in the Bible are to be admired, but not to the point where we idolize them or disbelieve that they were just like us. They served the same God we do today and were just as human and mistake prone as we are. We can also do the work of God in power and degrees as they did.

The Bible says, *"Not many wise men after the flesh, not many mighty, not many noble, are called: but God hath chosen the foolish things of the world to confound the wise; and God hath chosen the weak things of the war to confound the things which are mighty; and the base things of the world, and things which are despised, hath God chosen, yea, and things which are not, to bring to naught things that are: that no flesh should glory in his presence."* (1 Corinthians 1:26-29)

Our might does not begin in great exploits, but in our position in the body of Christ Jesus. In Him we are mighty because it is the Holy Spirit in us that makes us so through God. Realize that God has called us and can use any of us who has accepted Christ as their Savior and salvation. He did not rescue you and me from spiritual death to live common lives. God's plan is to have an intimate, loving relationship with us that leads to other intimate and loving relationships. Apart from Christ we can do nothing that will last. Outside of Christ, there is only existence and spiritual mediocrity. For us to deny this is truly to deny God in thought and deed.

Now that we know to be mighty is to have accepted salvation, we can move on to why we are not purposed to stand alone in this. Moses was so much like today's Christian in many ways. God had given him a people to lead not unlike some of us as teachers, fathers, mothers, and so on. Moses was trying to do it leaning on God, but humanly alone. This is not how

God ordained it to be. God gives us a plan and vision, but we must meditate with Him about how it looks beyond what our minds have imagined. No matter how small or great our sphere of influence is as child of a mighty of God, we are knit together with other members of the body of Christ. No Christian is low enough in sin or high enough in blessings to cease from being a part of the body of Christ. It is a lie to think we as Christians do not need one another. No matter how blessed or trial-filled the life a life of a Christian is, the whole body feels the joy and pain of it all. *"For as the body is one and hath many members and all the members of that one body, being many, are one body: so also, is Christ. And whether one member suffer, all the members suffer with it; or one member be honored, all the members rejoice with it."* (1 Corinthians 12:12,26).

Some reading this may have had a conversation with God like this:

You: I do not need anybody's help. Lord, your Word says I can do all through Christ Jesus who strengthens me. Interacting with people in your church at times seems to just makes things that much harder.

God: My child, how do you think I'm going to strengthen you to do ministry?

You: You will do it supernaturally by the Holy Spirit.

God: You are right, but I have placed my Holy Spirit in others as well as you so you can work together to accomplish my purpose. I did not call you to do everything by yourself.

You: Then why is it so hard to minister with others?

God: It is hard because they are just like you.

You: Just like me?

God: Yes. How much trouble do you have when dealing with yourself? I am the Head of this spiritual body. You cannot say you do not need the other parts but need me - we are one. When I send people into your life who rub you the wrong way, I want to you to turn to me for answers, so they do not continue to have that effect on you. You have turned away so many times and it is time that you stand and allow me to use others to perfect you.

In America, is not the nation affected if the president is ill? Is not the president affected if half of Congress is having problems in a specific area? Is not the whole executive branch of federal government affected if ten cities have major dilemmas? If you can see in this example how people depend on and are affected by others, how can you deny that you as a Christian aren't needy of one another's love and spiritual gifts?

The church needs each other. I am not talking about a building or committee (though these are useful parts of the church), but the spiritual body of individuals that make up the body of Christ. It matters not that we are committed to Jesus Christ if we stand alone while people who attend our church, who we have never spoken to or had fellowship with are having spiritual problems. We must serve them. If Christians ask for our help but we are always too busy to help, (even if it is with God's work), they will not grow in Christ because we are standing alone as Moses.

If we are fasting, praying, reading the Bible, and doing our best to be a disciple of Christ, while not sharing with others or witnessing about what God has done in our lives, we are trying to stand alone as Moses.

We cannot stand alone! We are a part of something bigger and a part is not strong or functional unless it is together with the whole. Unless we are sharing, fellowshipping, or teaching what God has taught us with others, we will be standing alone and even hindering the rest of the body.

"And Sampson said unto the lad that held him by the hand, suffer me that I may feel the pillars where upon the house standeth, that I may lean upon them." (Judges 16:26)

Mighty one, have your spiritual eyes been put out because of sin and iniquity? Have your feet been made lame because you would not obey God? Has your mind become heavy with the worries and burdens of life? God has heard your cries. Your sins that held you can be broken. If you will repent and ask God to cleanse and use you, He will do it. He did it for Sampson. He did it for David. He did it for the Samaritan woman at the well. He will do it for you too.

Never become arrogant and think you can stand alone outside of God or your brothers and sisters in Christ. *"Who art thou that judges another man's servant? To his master he standeth or falleth. Yea, he shall be holden up: for God is able to make him stand."* (Romans 14:4) *"Wherefore let him that thinketh he standeth take heed lest he fall."* (1 Corinthians 10:12)

Saul was a man anointed by God but because of his disobedience and standing alone, he lost his joy and kingdom. No man standeth unless God allows it.

The pessimistic Christian may question if God would allow evil individuals to stand. Not to burst the bubbles of those who do not think evil can be allowed by God to accomplish his will, but for the sake of truth I must. We need to understand that all things were created by God for his purposes and just because society does not deem it appropriate means nothing, *"The Lord hath made all things for himself: yea, and the wicked for the day of evil."* (Proverbs 16:4)

Saul lost his dependence on God toward the end of his life. The sin and high-mindedness in his life walled him in from hearing God's voice, *"And when Saul inquired of the Lord, he answered him not, neither by dreams, nor by Urim, nor by prophets. Then said Saul unto his servants, Seek me a woman that hath a familiar spirit, that I may go to her, and inquire of her. "* (1 Samuel 28:6-7)

Mighty one of God, have you not heard the voice of God in your life? Do you take note of it now and realize it is because of sin or not leaning upon God in prayer? Do not seek God as Saul did. God is a God to be waited patiently upon. How can you stand with God's help when you never wait long enough in prayer to hear Him? When we go to God in prayer, we must understand his heart. He is our father and has a heart that knows exactly what we need, *"But where sin abounded, grace did much more abound."* (Romans 5:20)

God has allowed us to face some situations to face us so we could not stand alone. Cry out and believe God will hear and answer you as a father answers the cries of his child.

Now I speak to anyone who has not depended upon God enough to even give your life to Him. *"Now we know that God heareth not sinners: but if any man be a worshipper of God, and doeth his will, him he heareth."* (John 9:31)

Give God authority in your life. Satan has robbed you long enough. Stop struggling and striving to figure out life and God through self-will and self-determination. Take Jesus' yoke upon you for it is light. The rest you need is found in standing boldly in Christ as a new creature. Come out of the selfish, wearisome shackles of self. Go boldly before God's throne and share where you hid and bear fruit where you were once fruitless.

In Jesus' name I tell you, you cannot be mighty and stand alone. Christ needed the Father, David needed Jonathan, you need me, and I need you. You are here to stand with others and God. Does a coal burn long when separated from the fire? Does fruit grow unless it abides on the tree? No Christian apart from God can do anything, nor can they grow properly outside of the body of Christ. *"And the eye cannot say unto the hand, I have no need of thee: nor again the head to the feet, I have no need of you."* (1 Corinthians 12:21)

Every single one of you who call on the name of Jesus Christ as Lord is mighty and needed as a part of the spiritual body.

Take a minute to read John 6:1-9. If the lad mentioned in this scripture had not been present, this miracle would have gone undone. If Andrew had not spoken up and found the lad, the miracle would have gone undone.

Now flip to Nehemiah and read the chapter. These men the scripture references were only doing the work God made them capable of. Their names are now written in the Bible as a testament to their individual work that created a piece of a whole work of God.

Do not tell me other people can stand without us or vice versa. You are an important piece of the body of Christ and in your lifetime, you can find a place to fit that was only missing you. Every created thing depends on something else. The mighty can't stand

alone.

Chapter 4
One Man's Trash Is Another Man's Treasure

What do you see in a five-dollar bill? A child may see something to play with or a start towards the amount they need to purchase something. A poor person may see a meal or blessing from God. A drug dealer may see a way to make double. An established businessperson may see what they once considered a beginning to now be an inconsequential item that can be passed by or stepped on because they no longer deal in small currency but large lump sums.

Have you ever viewed a colony of ants around a trashcan? They march in the filthiest of areas and come out with sustenance for the future. We as men and women of God need to realize as God told Peter, *"...what God hath cleansed, that call not thou common."* (Acts 10:15)

We as followers of Christ Jesus need to reflect how God has so many times taken what some considered trash and used it as another's treasure to help others.

For the preaching of the cross is to them that perish foolishness; but unto us which are saved, it is the power of God. For after that in wisdom of God the world by wisdom knew not God, it pleased God by the foolishness of preaching to save them that believe. But we preach Christ crucified, unto the Jews a stumbling block, and unto the Greeks foolishness; but unto them which were called, both Jews and Greeks, Christ the power of God, and the wisdom of God. Because the foolishness of God is wiser than men; and the weakness of God is stronger than men." (1 Corinthians 1:18, 21, 23-25).

Take note of how Paul tells us that men perishing consider Christ on the cross foolishness or a stumbling block. How many times have you been witnessing about the goodness and power of God only to have questions about Christ on the cross, the color of Christ's skin, or why so many Christians are fake derail the conversation? Even if what is meant to be a serious conversation is derailed, know that the pearls of your witness have not been in vain. What the "listener" may see as garbage is a seed that has been planted.

In Paul's day, the cross and Christ dying on it was considered trash to the religious and philosophical elite. However, to the oppressed and poor who searched for the Christ in spirit and in truth, the crucifixion was the atonement of sin, fulfillment of prophecy, and justification of God's chosen people. The Gentiles (because of the Jews' unbelief and God's grace) had a door opened to them.

Our nation today is one not unlike those of ancient times. The chariot has been replaced by the car and messengers have been replaced by more efficient modes of communication, but there are still key similarities such as: God's unchanging character, good versus evil, and the treasures of God being blindly discarded by people for the trash of this world.

The Bible says in Luke 16:11, *"If therefore ye have not been faithful in the unrighteousness mammon, who will commit to your trust the true riches?"*

The point of the scripture is that money and the cares of this world are everything to man but nothing to God. While it is good and a blessing to be financially secure and have responsibilities, can you imagine trying to convince God to let you into heaven because you were wealthy or did a great job carrying out civic duties?

God puts supreme value on faith in Hebrews 11:6, *"But without faith it is impossible to please him: for he that cometh to God must believe that he is, and that he is a rewarder of them that diligently seek him."*

Anything done without faith in God is trash before God, *"But we are all as an unclean thing, and all our righteousness's are as filthy rags..."* (Isaiah 64:6)

God looks at the heart of who an individual is. A person who puts their faith in Jesus Christ and is bearing the fruit of the Spirit in their life (Galatians 5:22-23) is one who will enter the kingdom of heaven with rewards waiting. To prove this point, the Spirit has led me to contrast how what man considers worthless at times is a treasure of God's omniscient will such as found in Judges 15:15-17, *"And he found a new jawbone of an ass, and put forth his hand, and took it, and slew a thousand men therewith. And Samson said, with the jawbone of an ass, heaps upon heaps, with the jawbone of an ass have I slain a thousand men. And it came to pass when he had made an end of speaking, that he cast away the jawbone out of his hand and called that place Ramathlehi."*

Consider an old and bedraggled church that sits on the street corner. Some might think it should be destroyed and have something bigger, better, and newer built in its place that would be of use to the neighborhood. Afterall, what good is that building as it is now? To the now grown child who found community for themselves and their single mom during a difficult time just a few years earlier, it was a sign from God that they were going to make it. It was life giving. Perspective can change everything.

Now who would have conceived that a jawbone of an ass would become a decisive weapon and a namesake for a place. Sampson, not only defeated sword, spear, and man with a jawbone of an ass, but named a whole place after the weapon he uses (Ramathlehi means the high place of the jawbone). God's Word says, *"All things work together for good to them that love God."* (Romans 8:28)

God in his omnipotent knowledge of events allowed the jawbone to be at that place for that particular purpose. People having passed by the jawbone by considering it trash did not change the value of the jawbone to Sampson and God's will.

Do you feel like the jawbone knowing you have value and purpose, but needing God and someone else to bring it out and use it to accomplish something great? Realize that God took a non-thinking, non-feeling object and used it to destroy some of his enemies and name a place. How much more will God use you? Just live in God's will and watch for opportunities and others to enter your life and help you achieve your purpose.

You don't have to search or strive to show how valuable God made you. As David said, *"Wait on the Lord, and keep his way, and he shall exalt thee to inherit the land."* (Psalm 37:24)

We are the fruit of Christ. Fruit does not toil or work but abides, grows, and matures into its purpose as God deems it. (To read more on this subject, see

John 15:1-11.) People's treasures are often found in "trash" as need and circumstances arise, and they seek godly wisdom to understand their true value. Who would have thought that discarded, disheartened, damaged people could be used by a perfect God? Look in the mirror. When you came to accept Jesus Christ into your heart, what did he see in the mirror? Look what the Lord has done.

"And Elisha said unto her, what shall I do for her? Tell me, what hast thou in the house? And she said, hand maid bath not anything in the house, save a pot of oil. Then he said, Go, borrow thee vessels abroad of all thy neighbors, even empty vessels; borrow not a few." (2 Kings 4:2-3, 7)

Have you ever felt cornered in certain areas of your life? You may have had bills to pay with only one dollar to your name. You may have been asked questions about God but only had one testimony to answer or needed to do five things and only have thirty minutes to do them in. I've been there.

Know the seemingly inconsequential, often ignored act of obedience to the voice of God will open the windows of heaven to you. God says in Malachi 3:10, *"Bring ye all the tithes into the storehouse, that there may be meat in my house, and prove me now herewith, saith the Lord of host, if I will not open you the windows of heaven, and pour you out a blessing, that there shall not be room enough to receive it.'*

The widow God blessed through the oil made a request on Elisha and then she hearkened and obeyed the word of God that came through Elisha and was blessed.

Our society has taken obedience and reverence for God and made it seem like trash. This is a tactic of Satan to get godly people to walk in rebellion against God. Throughout God's Word, we see Him saying obedience is better than sacrifice. Obedience is a treasure to a godly man. Only through obedience to God do we truly submit and show our love for Him. Society tells us "To pray without ceasing, conquer and break bad habits and addictions, and be Christ like in everyday lives," is too much for anyone. This is a lie from Satan! The world tells Christians about how to supposedly live a fulfilled life while behind closed doors they live unsatisfied, confused, and deficient lives.

God said we can do all things in and through Christ (Philippians 4:13). If we walk in obedience of his statutes and expectations and stand in reverence of his power and mercy, we can be free in Him. God treasures obedience in his children and the world hates us and Him for it. *"Wherein they think it strange that ye run not with them to the same excess of riot, speaking evil of you."* (1 Peter 4:4)

God said and creation obeyed. Jesus said and death obeyed. Now God says and it is up to you and me to obey. Will you consider obedience to God's Word trash or treasure? Which will be a jewel in your crown of life? It is obvious that the world's trash can be God's treasures. Though we may not understand we should always defer our judgment to Lord's Word: *"And God saw everything that he made, and behold, 'It was very GOOD."* (Genesis 1:31)

What if you doubt your self-worth? The key is to remember that your worth and value is defined by God's use and purpose, not man's opinion. The world has a cruel but accepted way of telling people through channels such as ads and social media that if you own this, look like this, or do that, you will be worth more to yourself and others. This is not true. Your worth is found in Christ. You cannot just ask questions and watch others to truly ascertain what it means to be a Christian. Psalm 34:8 says, *"O taste and see that the Lord is good."*

Realize that doubt of your self-worth does not stem from failures, but from the fact that you do not know who you are in Christ. Either Satan has lied and said you are trash and not treasure or you have not accepted salvation.

Those who have been saved can hold fast to 2 Corinthians 5:17 which says, *"Therefore if any man be in Christ, he is a new creature: old things are passed away; behold, all things are become new."*

Those that are not yet saved should remember that as a creation of God you are already special, but nothing compared to who God wants you to be in Christ. The difference between the saved and unsaved is a choice. Are God's promises of salvation trash or treasure to you? Words are not needed to answer this question because your acceptance or rejection of Jesus Christ as your Lord and Savior speaks volumes of your view of God (trash or treasure).

There is a story that begins in Luke 10:30 that illustrates how even when others may not recognize and appreciate you, God does. In this parable, a lawyer questions Jesus about who his neighbor is and if he should love them as himself. In reply, Jesus tells of a man who fell among thieves and was left for dead. A priest and a Levite saw the man but did not render help. A Samaritan stopped and helped the man despite the fact he was from Jerusalem (Samaritans did not get along with people from Jerusalem and vice versa). Notice that the priest and the Levite who should have found value in the man's life did not, but instead the man's enemy chose compassion for the man.

For centuries this world has dictated that affluence, race, denomination, and literacy define what you and I consider trash and treasure, but God does not see these things. God has given us his Word and Spirit and asks us to care for and help all who callout to God. Know there are some of us who lay on the side of the road spiritually. I want you to know- you are not alone. God knows just what you need, but you must stop looking through the world's stereotypes and instead look to God's prototype. Find the guidance and counsel of someone who has laid down their life for God, picked up their cross, and is willing to crucify, themselves daily to the world and self. They can help you see yourself the way God sees you- a treasure and a diamond in the rough.

I use the word trash because though it sounds harsh, it is an accurate reflection of society's viewpoints about self, others, and God. In this view, trash is something unusable or already used up. When adopting this view to talk about God, it may sound like this:

- I don't believe in God.
- I don't need God.
- I tried God and He didn't work.

Yet, everything God makes has a hidden treasure or value- even evil:

"The Lord bath made all things for himself: yea, even the wicked for the day of evil." (Proverbs 16:4)

"But in a great house there are not only vessels of gold and of silver, but also of wood and of earth, and some to honor, end some to dishonor." (2 Timothy 2:20)

There will be times when we must lean on others who give of their treasure so we can in turn give of our treasure to others. This is how God's creation works. Afterall, who do bees make honey for? They don't eat it! Who do trees bear fruit for? Not for themselves.

Our best attributes should be for others and not ourselves. All that we say, do, and think should help others grow and realize their value to and in God. True treasure is something to be unconditionally shared and beneficial to all.

Trash is merely you or I not utilizing all God has given us to glorify and honor Him. Your choices will determine what is trash and treasure in your life. One person's trash is another's treasure because of choices.

What does the Bible say about treasure? In Luke 12 beginning in verse 16, Jesus tells a parable of a rich man who had plenty. The man decided to build greater barns than what he had, because of this plenty he would have for years to come. But in verses 20 and 21 God says, *"Thou fool this night thy soul shall be required of thee: then who's shall those things be, which thou hast provided? So is he that layeth up treasure for himself, and is not rich toward God?"*

A just man shall have basic needs such as clothes and food met, but righteousness and salvation are where everlasting treasures are found. In the Bible, Solomon, David, and Gideon were all given material wealth only after they first sought everlasting spiritual wealth. Yet, many a man has sadly traded morals for materialism thinking the latter is the bigger treasure. This way of thinking requires a new perspective because righteousness and salvation in Christ makes the wealth of the world pale in comparison.

God has enabled Christians to enjoy both kinds of wealth *for his purposes*. How we use these gifts will dictate whether they ultimately become trash or treasure for us. Our reverence for God has immense spiritual value and can shape our experiences with wealth.

In 1 Kings 17, God sends the prophet Elijah eastward to hide by the brook of Cherith where God promises he will receive drink and sustenance. It is important to note that God had already prepared sustenance for Elijah, but only after he reverently obeyed in duty and following instructions was, he able to access it. When you are given the tangible treasures of God's blessing, realize they are temporary and material and are only upheld by the spiritual blessings God has given you.

Elijah discovered the temporary nature of some blessings firsthand when the brook from which he drank dried up because there was no rain. The same blessings that upheld Elijah turned what had once been an oasis into dry and unyielding earth.

We must learn that God's treasures are not to be consumed on only ourselves. Some of us have stayed by the brook for too long. The treasures of God that once blessed us have now turned into death traps.

Staying by the brook of Cherith too long may look like a minister who once witnessed to ten people a day now having trouble finding an attentive ear. It may look like a young couple who once thrived at church now experiencing relationship problems because of family turmoil. Why? Because we cannot stay at Cherith forever and we must move on to where God directs us.

Our need to please God must be greater than our need to be comfortable. Moving is spiritual before it manifests physically. God has given you his Word to study and the Holy Spirit to guide us, but when we stop looking for the spiritual treasures of God, we begin accumulating spiritual trash. *"The backslider in heart shall be filled with his own ways: and a good man shall be satisfied from himself."* (Proverbs 14:14)

Think of it this way. Fire is a good thing to cook with, but when food is left over it too long, the fire becomes a destroyer. The temperature may not have changed in your life, but you have stood still too long. Daily seek God's face to find out what He wants you to do. Just because you have done one thing that has worked for some time, does not mean it always will. Growth is necessary.

In Acts 6:1-4, the disciples stayed in Jerusalem too long, and before long petty division and intense persecution took place:

And in those days, when the number of the disciples was multiplied, there arose a murmuring of the Grecians against the Hebrews, because their widows were neglected in the daily ministration. Then the twelve called the multitude of the disciples unto them, and said, it is not reason that we should leave the word of God and serve tables. Wherefore, brethren, look ye out among you seven men of honest report, full of the Holy Ghost and wisdom, whom we may appoint over this business. But we will give ourselves continually to prayer, and to the ministry of the word."

Put the treasure of a Spirit-led life ahead of tradition and material items and see how Matthew 6:33 is a promise for those who claim and live it. Good intentions don't handle or excuse disobedience.

Are your treasures in heaven? What have you claimed as treasure through God's Word? And how can you store more treasure in heaven for eternity? The Bible clearly outlines what treasures are to be claimed and how to claim them.

Do not focus on what you have; focus on how you achieved it in Christ. Living in Christ is the only way you can truly recognize and purposefully use treasure. What can you gain for God's kingdom today? What can you give that will remain?

Chapter 5
A Word of Manna
(Potluck Style)

There are times in the course of being a Christian that you will have special needs that go far beyond the resources that are available where you are. This chapter is devoted to meeting those needs this present day in your life. Only God knows the needs and words you need.

Paul said that he waited, submitted, was torn down and built up, and humbled himself all to have the opportunity and resources to make a difference for Christ in others' lives. Though Christ is sovereign over all things, to be a difference maker for God we must be a difference maker to his people.

So many times, applause is given for a minister who stirs up the emotions of the people but not the spirit of the people. This book was not written to please man, but to serve God. My heart cries out to God every time his Word goes forth in power. It's an awesome experience to know God is talking to you through his Word--albeit through a minister's or teacher's lips. Many people function in the capacity of teacher and preacher, but only a few properly present God's messages with the passion, emotion, and mannerisms God knows his people need to see and hear to pay attention to and grasp the message.

How many times have you gone to a church and left feeling like the minister preached liked no one else you have heard? Probably not often! Why? Because the Word of God is the same worldwide but the love, dedication, and obedience of those who deliver it are different. This chapter is devoted to sharing the power, love, and goodness of God.

"Then said the Lord unto Moses, Behold, I will rain bread from heaven for you; and the people shall go out and gather a certain rate every day, that I may prove them, whether they will walk in my law or no. And when they did mete it with an omer, he that gathered much had nothing over, and he that gathered little had no lack; they gathered every man according to his eating. And Moses said, let no man leave of it till morning. Notwithstanding they hearkened not unto Moses; but none of them left of it until the morning, and

it bred worms, and stank: and Moses was wroth with them." (Exodus 16:4,18-20)

This chapter is designed to immediately be implemented into your life. To the reader who is walking in power of Christ, this chapter will affirm and further your understanding of him. To the lukewarm Christian, this chapter will cut and heal the mediocre parts of your life. To the self-righteous or low-esteemed Christian, this chapter will bring to the surface any feelings of pride or fear- give them up to God as He reveals them to you. Finally, to the newly converted Christian, this chapter will give you goals and expectations from the Spirit for your life.

I never did quite grasp the concept of a potluck dinner. I have been to a few and although they always smelled and tasted good, it bewildered me how one could throw things in a pot that normally didn't go together and still come out with a delicious meal. I don't care where you're from, or how finicky your appetite- with the right seasoning and fresh ingredients, you will enjoy it.

The ingredients for this chapter are meat (the Word of God); seasoning- (the anointing of God), and water (the Living Water of the Holy Spirit). Do not be overly concerned about calories for these ingredients are God approved and recommended.

"Labor not for the meat which perisheth, but for that meat which endureth unto everlasting life, which the Son of Man shall give unto you: for him hath God the Father sealed. Then Jesus said unto them, Verily, Verily, I say unto you, Moses gave you not that bread from heaven; but my Father giveth you the true bread from heaven. For the bread of God is he which cometh

down from heaven, and giveth life unto the world." (John 6:27, 32-33)

God knows that sometimes you need an assortment of ingredients to handle one certain recipe for life. This chapter gives you sample bites of different subjects that all mingle together to satisfy the ravenous hunger that exists in your soul and help you be a better follower of Christ.

Famine

Christians should serve others by bearing one another's burdens and praying, but to undertake these ministries on an empty spiritual stomach is dangerous. Problems arise when a Christian does not fill up on the things God gives to sustain and nourish them.

In everything you do your body must be properly rested and fed to yield optimum performance. Imagine trying to run a marathon when your body is already malnourished before the race ever begins. Serving God is no different. Even Christ made time to be nourished by God (Luke 22:41). We must pay close attention to how we fill ourselves up because the devil waits for opportunities when he sees us spiritually malnourished. This is exhibited beautifully in Matthew 4:4 when Satan tempts Jesus to change stones to bread. Jesus responds by saying, *"Man shall not live by bread alone, but by every word that proceedeth out of the mouth of God."*

Hope Famine

"And Abraham rose up early in the morning, and took bread, and a bottle of water, and gave it unto Hagar, putting it on her shoulder, and the child, and

sent her away: and she departed, and wandered in the wilderness of Beersheba." (Genesis 21:14)

You have accepted Jesus Christ as your Lord and Savior. You finally chose to serve God and others more than self. You have the indwelling of the Holy Spirit to teach you and Jesus Christ to love you. The world suddenly seems a little brighter, but also so much harder now.

The words you once said and lived by are taboo. The friends you partied and sometimes had sex with no longer want you around. The newfound lifestyle you are living has you feeling lonely, desperate, and unsure of yourself. Good! Now you are ready for your miracle. Pleasing God is going to feel and, at times, look different than pleasing self. Some days you may feel alone but are being blessed by spending time in the presence of your God versus enjoying the wrong kind of company that will do you no good.

Satan was captain and he had you on a suicide mission to hell. Hagar, had to feel the same way. She had been a good handmaid to Sarah. She was chosen to bring forth a child to Abram for Sarah. She became pregnant and had the child, Ishmael. I know Hagar expected a good life to follow, but God had other plans. Soon after, Sarah bore a son named Isaac and told Abraham to put Hagar and Ishmael out of the house.

We can think we have made it with a great new job in a new city and no more struggling financially or living paycheck to paycheck. We think all the sacrifices we have made have paid off, but what about the ministry your pastor told you about? The one that could really use someone like you. While true that the pay may not be as competitive as you might like, you would be helping so many. What about that opportunity?

Sadly, many new converts in Christ as well as Christians who have had salvation for years have made no evident changes or growth since accepting Christ as Lord. They had or have skyscraper-like expectations of living a life for God, but daily make decisions with no thought of what God wants for them. These people have valid expectations but must realize that to build a skyscraper takes time, a good foundation, and a bottom floor.

"And the water was spent in the bottle, and she cast the child under one of the shrubs. And she went and sat her down over against him a good way off, as it were a bow shot: for she said, Let me not see the death of the child." (Genesis 21:15-16a)

Hagar, it seems, had become destitute of hope. I'm sure when she was carrying Abram's baby, she had ideas of how her social status would greatly improve.

People would see her and remember her past as a slave but esteem her as the woman who helped carry Abram's family name forward. Even when she was despised by Sarah during her pregnancy and ran away in Genesis 16, the angel of the Lord appeared and gave her a prophecy to hope in. But now she sat thirsty and desperate with no hope of survival as she waited for her young child to die.

Today many Christians sit at church, go to work daily, and compromise with the world waiting to die. They have been maligned for their faith, disappointed by church leadership, and unsatisfied with sacrifices that living a holy life for God requires. As a result, they just exist. Outwardly they say how blessed they are and flaunt WWJD bumper stickers, but inwardly they are envious of the sin's others seem to be enjoy committing.

This is how Hagar likely felt. She was favored, blessed, and being taken care of by God, but she lacked in giving God her time, resources, and self. God gave Hager a promise in Genesis 16:10 that He would "multiply thy seed exceedingly," but after He made that promise, she stopped giving God her worship.

Jesus gave us the promise in John 10:10, *"I am come that they might have life, and that they might have it more abundantly."* Many of us have believed this promise but failed to spend quality time alone with God to experience it. God gives hope to all who hear and obey what He says. The famine of hope in Hagar and in some Christians today is rooted in the fact that we have not continued to spend time with God so He could sustain the hope He gives us through his Word. Without a daily hearing, reading, and praying of the Word, we will eventually experience a famine of hope.

The answer to a famine of hope is to get a word from God about your circumstances. Once you receive this word you must abide in, believe, and obey it. To live any other way as a child of God is to live on a spiritual crumb. You may think you can survive on crumbs and find joy in maintaining appearances in this life, but Jesus wants us to live abundantly every day. To live abundantly is to live intimately in communion with God every day despite our circumstances.

"And he said, A certain man had two sons: And the younger of them said to his father, Father, give me the portion of goods that falleth to me. And he divided unto them his living. And not many days after the younger son gathered all together and took his journey into a far country." (Luke 15:11-13)

Two are better than one. Two feet. Two hands. Two cars. Even God told Adam it was not good for him to be alone. There are Christians reading this book who like the company of people, but not necessarily that of other believers. How could this be possible? Simple. Most people do not want to be held accountable to a higher standard than the one they establish for themselves. They do not want those who think they live recklessly to intervene. There can be a misplaced feeling of safety in keeping company with nonbelievers because they do not care if you are living destructively as it does not impact them.

Know this: believers fellowshipping one with another is based upon Jesus Christ being the connector. This is one of the wonders of this world. Put people whose Savior is Jesus Christ and whose life is focused on living in an intimate and obedient relationship with Jesus Christ all in the same room, and you will see a dynamic and diverse family.

But even this type of family can have struggles and disagreements. Many times, this is a result of people not having peace within themselves, much less with each other. However, as believers grow in knowledge and love, they come to understand it takes work to commit to loving relationships. The work is not in establishing the relationships (because Jesus does that), but in living out the commitment to the Christian family despite different dynamics.

When believers choose to sever relationships with other believers, they will find themselves in a secluded spiritual existence and a downward spiral of spiritual famine. God can use the family of God to protect you and me from the world and ourselves. Protection may sometimes feel like being restricted from some things like sex before marriage, drug usage, and other sinful behaviors that in the sight of God are roads leading to a wasted life.

Examine your life. How fulfilled are you? Are you working at a job that brings you contentment? How much value do you place on the relationships you are striving to keep?

Come home. The Church (body of believers in Jesus Christ) is here for you just as the prodigal son in Luke 15:17-24 who returns humbly to his father after going astray and is welcomed back whole heartedly. You have not been called to serve God out of fellowship with other believers. Your strength is maximized in the context of fellowship with other believers. Really look at what passion and talents were given to you. Your life is not just for you. God has always had a plan for it. You are at your best in the midst of His people. Your hidden worst can be healthily exposed and dealt with in godly fellowship. When

God's people see a person's worst, they should correct, minister, and understand. Nobody who has not had to face God concerning their sin can truly understand the capacity of His forgiveness, grace, and mercy.

You began in Christ who brought you into the family of God. This family has a rich history, promising future, and a perfect father. It also has relatives with problems and issues. As a member of the body of Christ you were given the Holy Spirit to help and lead you. He is the one who you can trust to help you know right from wrong, navigate different seasons of life, and empower you to grow as a part of the body of Christ.

No Holy Ghost Power

"And when he came to his disciples, he saw a great multitude about them, and the scribes

questioning with them. And straightway all the people, when they beheld him, were greatly amazed, and running to him saluted him. And he asked the scribes, What question ye with them? And one of the multitude answered and said, Master, I have brought unto thee my son, which hath a dumb spirit; And where so ever he taketh him, he teareth him: and he foameth, and gnasheth with his teeth, and pineth away: and I spake to thy disciples that they should cast him out; and they could not. (Mark 9:14-18)

Where are the miracles that God use to do? Has someone in the last fifty years walked into a hospital and healed all the sick people? It seems in our day and time that in America the church must make excuses for God not doing many miracles.

God still does miracles. Show me the life of someone who's living a trusting-obedient life to God. That is a miracle to me. Lives that had been destroyed by drugs are now restored. Minds that had been confused and suicidal over lost love are now at peace. Incarcerated men and women are ministering to one another while serving decades behind bars. Illnesses are being diagnosed as terminal, but patients go on to live decades before they die. Sexually abused people who have lived are helping others and forgiving their abusers. People who have been taken advantage of by someone close are now finding strength to forgive. These are miracles.

Jesus' disciples who had done this type of ministry before in Mark 6:7-13 found themselves lacking in the ability to exercise authority over a dumb and death spirit. How could this happen? The disciples were called up and believed they could help but could not meet the need. It was not due to a lack of faith on their part, it was components their lifestyle was lacking, the reason was. lack of lifestyle by the disciples. *"And he said unto them, this kind can come forth by nothing, but by prayer and fasting."* (Mark 9:29)

Jesus was not telling the disciples that when they were presented with the boy they should have ran away, fasted, and prayed and then returned. He was telling them that if they had been living a regular lifestyle of prayer and fasting then they would have had the active power to cast out the evil spirit. The disciples had walked in this active power before but had not maintained the disciplines of regular prayer and fasting.

Prayer and fasting keep us aware and involved with God in the unseen spiritual realm. People today have a famine of the power of the Holy Spirit because they do not stay intimate with God in the way the Bible instructs. We do our own thing and want God to join in. If you are a believer in Jesus Christ, you know that when trouble hits you want the Holy Spirit's help. To be baptized in the Holy Spirit is to be fully immersed and empowered by Him. It is to let Him work through you and show you the part you play.

When it comes to matters of employment, finance, church affiliation, and relationships, most of us never consider what the Holy Spirit is saying to us. When it comes to terminal illnesses such as cancer or life and death surgeries, we are suddenly ready, willing, and desperate enough to believe in Him and listen to Him too. To truly live in the power of the Holy Spirit we must live a LIFE where the Holy Spirit is in charge not just part time, but all of the time.

Having the power of the Holy Spirit seals your salvation in Christ. The baptism of the Holy Spirit is to equip you for the work of edifying the body of Christ. A good example of this truth is if you read Galatians 5:22-23 and compare it to 1 Corinthians 12:4-11. The scripture in Galatians talks about the fruit of the Spirit and how it can make us more like Christ. The scripture in 1 Corinthians acknowledges that we may have different gifts, but all are given by the same Spirit.

Many Christians are trying to do things for God of and through themselves. It is the power of the Holy Ghost that works in us to walk and work for God in power and authority. Have you ever wondered why two Christians can sing the same song but only one of them experiences the Holy Spirit stirring to life? It is the power of the Holy Ghost.

Have you ever witnessed a man speak for an hour out of the Bible and nothing is stirred in you, but another stands up, offers one scripture, expounds on it 15 minutes, and you are left changed for a lifetime? It is the power of the Holy Ghost.

People in this day and time want to make a difference for God. They want to see the results of working fervently for God. Unfortunately, it is not the majority but the minority that is doing it. Still, a bright light is that mighty revival can take place when there is already a small fire burning.

The disciples needed and were commanded to wait for power. I know Christians today who have a heart for God's work but will not ask for the power of baptism of the Holy Ghost because they have not heard of it or do not understand it. The disciples did not understand, but they waited on it.

God only gives good gifts. Ask Him for something good, in faith, and you will get it if it is according to His will. The disciples had walked in power before, but never consistently. If you read the first five chapters of Acts, you will see a drastic change in the apostles' character and witness. This was not to their credit except in that they were obedient to Jesus' command to wait on power.

I know right now there are people who want to move in boldness and authority. God tells them to, but they are not. All you must do is ask God for this power.

To readers who doubt baptism of the Holy Ghost, I pose this viewpoint: If you ask God out of a pure heart and the right motive for something that does not exist, why would you be punished? But if you do not ask God for what is truly beneficial for you and the church, wouldn't you be held accountable for not using all God gave you to do its work?

When Jesus comes back, will you be rebuked that you read and didn't respond in faith in God? "Yet ye have not, because you ask not." (James 4:2)

Have You Learned?

"And we know that all things work together for good: to them that love God, to them who are the called according to is purpose." (Romans 8:28)

God, in His sovereignty, works all experiences in a Christian's life to bring to arrive at His appointed goal. Oftentimes because of our lack of seeking God's face to understand our trials, we miss the value in them. The question that I pose to you today is, "Have you learned from your past and present trials to better handle your problems of today and tomorrow?

I discussed Jacob in an earlier chapter. In the waiting years of Jacob's life, his experiences with the Lord became a blueprint for him to handle problems Lord's way. In chapter 32 of Genesis, we see Jacob tried to buy peace with Esau but when it did not work, he prayed to God for help. Jacob was a man accustomed to doing things his name (which means supplanted or trickster) said he would. A self-willed, head-strong Christian must learn that the life of a Christian is about stewardship over what God entrusts us with, not serving self.

"And their father Israel (Jacob) said unto them, it must be so now, do this; take of the best fruits in the land in your purses and carry down the present, a little balm, and a little honey, spices and myrrh, nuts and almonds. Take also your brother, and arise, go again unto the man: and God Almighty give you mercy before the man, that he may send away your other brother, and Benjamin. If I be bereaved of my children, I am bereaved." (Genesis 43:11, 13-14)

Here Israel (Jacob) found himself faced with another life altering decision. This time rather than be a manipulator, he prepared material presents to gain favor from an individual. He was resigned to accept the Lord's help and decision on the whole matter. This may seem like a small change in the character of Israel (Jacob) by him saying, *"If I be bereaved of my children,*

I am bereaved," but it is as significant as Jesus saying, "Nevertheless, not my will, but thane, be done." (Luke 22:42)

Every mighty person of God, know that your patience, perseverance, and experiences are to mature you so you can tell God and mean it, "Not my will, but yours." If you reflect upon decisions in your life, you can attest to the fact that leaning on yourself has only left you hurt, empty, lonely, or all three. God wants you to reach the point where you know how good He is and trust his will for your life instead of your circumstances and worldly wisdom.

Worldly thinking would have kept Jesus from the cross—for how could one man's death save all who believed and called upon his name? Worldly thinking would have kept the disciples from going out to the different parts of the world preaching about Jesus—for how could a few men cause people to believe in the span of 30 something years a man could change the world forever and for good?

Do not be deceived by the good intentions of this world toward common sense thinking. Good intentions and manners will not get you to heaven, but salvation and turning your life decisions over to God will get you there and bless in this earthly life also. If you have not learned to depend upon God, then more turbulent times lay ahead. Putting trust in God does not mean bad things won't occur in your life.

"If it be so, our God whom we serve is able to deliver us from the burning fiery furnace and he will deliver us out of thine hand king. But if riot, be it known unto thee, O king that we will not serve thy gods." (Daniel 3:17-18)

The Hebrew boys Shadrach, Meshach, and Abednego knew God was able to deliver them from the fire that Nebuchadnezzar was about to throw them in. They also knew that sometimes God used death to bring victories for Him also. They simply wanted what God wanted knowing that the God they served knew better than they the purpose for their lives. In the end, God allowed these boys to be thrown into the fire, but they came out unharmed in Daniel 3:19-30.

Do you know the perfect purpose God has for your life? Do you believe in the goodness of God? Have you learned from your own experiences or the preaching of God's Word that He loves us, knows what is best for us, and wants our faith to be in Him? It can be easy to say yes but before you do, think about what your furnace is today. Is it to change jobs or churches for your growth in doing God's work? Is it a decision to accept Jesus as Lord over the world? Or could it be just to trust God enough to let him be you be-all and end-all? No matter what your furnace is, realize that God is that best refiner of them all. God will never burn or reshape what doesn't need to be burned or reshaped and He will never lead you into or put you through a fire that is not useful to His will and your growth. Remain faithful to God because this is truly learning of God.

Self-Esteem

Many a problem crosses the lines society has drawn such as prejudice, conformity, and jealousy, but one problem exists that is crucial to the success or demise of Christians—self-esteem. Some men such as David were blessed to walk in the full authority of it, while others such as the Pharisees and Sadducees suffered from too much of it.

Self-esteem for the Christian is knowing who you are in Christ and what you were created to do. You will never know the full extent of your influence on others. You may plant and water the seeds of God's Word, but God gives the increase. Perhaps you will be blessed to see this increase, but often you will not see it all. Christians are meant to touch others' lives for God, but first they must be touched themselves by God.

"Leah was tender eyed: but Rachel was beautiful an. well-favored. And (Jacob) want in also unto Rachel, and he loved also Rachel more than Leah, and served with him (Laban) yet seven other years. And when the Lord saw that Leah was hated, he opened her womb: but Rachel was barren." (Genesis 29:17,30-31)

Do not let the gender of this story cause you to discount the relevant lessons that can be applied to you. Both women and men can learn something about the character of God from this passage.

Ladies, know that God sees your troublesome marriage and/or frustration in a relationship that lacks the full commitment of your boyfriend. He also sees your heart and the motives behind your involvement in this relationship. Stop looking for the passion, love, and companionship of a man, before you get it from God. Satan loves to use the tactics of age, loneliness, and low self-esteem to attract you to men who give you promises of what you dream of but never the realty of a covenant relationship.

Leah was not preferred and not the fairest in terms of physical attraction, but because she remained faithful to the covenant of marriage, God blessed her. Another woman may have taken your man, but they cannot take your faithfulness to God. *"But without faith it is impossible to please him for he that cometh to God must believe that he is, and that he is a rewarder of them that diligently seek him."* (Hebrews 11:6)

Leah's blessings were not dependent on Jacob's love, respect, or value of her. She was blessed because as a child of God she meant something special to God. You also mean something special to God with or without approval of your peers, family, or mate. Stop letting Satan manipulate you into emotional situations where your self-worth is determined by the opinions of others. You are who God says you are. Your feelings concerning your value are not as informed as God's are. You are who God made you.

Whether you feel like a million dollars, or an emotional wreck does not change who you are in Christ. When you look in God's Word and thank God for revealing your identity, rest and peace on the inside are just some of the rewards.

Men, in many aspects how Leah was treated is how we treat one another. If we cannot find the benefits or feelings we want in superficial ways from others, we discard them and move on. Realize that and know some of the things you have discarded such as chastity and morals are still commanded and rewarded by God. We men of this day have become modern day a Jacob or Balaam. *"But I have a few things against thee, because thou hast there them that hold the doctrine of Balaam, who taught Balak to cast a stumbling block before the children of Israel, to eat things sacrificed unto idols, and to commit fornication."* (Revelation 2:14)

Not only have we forgotten and belittled the Leah of this present age, but we have used, insulted, oppressed, disrespected, and misled God's people with our behavior and attitudes. This is not an attack on men. I'm merely unfolding the truth that for us to recognize what we have done to women's self-esteem is to recognize where our own self-esteem has been. We cannot begin to build up a woman's self-esteem until we understand our own has been misplaced. Where is righteousness and courage as David had or obedience as Samuel had or the humility Christ had? We must pick up the pieces of our lives and turn them over to God to reshape and utilize us.

"And I, brethren, when I came to you, came not with excellency of speech or of wisdom, declaring unto you the testimony of God. For I determined not to know anything among you, save Jesus Christ, and him crucified." (1 Corinthians 2:1-2)

We must realize that it is not us who will lead, teach, or do any other good thing. It is Christ in us. We must stop putting pressure and glory on self and lean and praise God for using us. Glory not in the past or in what you felt was a success but was outside of Christ. Only what is of God will affirm the things of God. You cannot keep walking as a man of God if drawing your self-esteem from the things of this world.

Do not be fooled by the complexity in scheme but simplicity in practice of Satan's devices. Satan's game plan is simply to get you to sin, lean on self, and depend upon only what you can see to fight him, if you even recognize him at all. Though Satan tries to accomplish this in many ways, the purpose is always the same.

Trust in God in all that you do and even your mistakes will be steps to greater blessings. How can you abound if you have never begin abased? Who you are is not something you wrestle with and strive for? Who you are is who Christ made you to be, a child of God that seeks and obeys God's voice?

How many times have you obeyed God's voice not knowing what was next and seen the goodness and blessings of God come about? An example would be when the angel of the Lord told Philip in Acts 8:26 to, "Go 'toward the south, unto the way that goeth down from Jerusalem unto Gaza, which is desert."

From Philip's obedience, a man and accepted Christ into his life and was baptized. You must not ever think your knowledge or lack of about God or a certain situation will stop God from using you according to his will (see Proverbs 3:5-6).

Another good example of a man with high self-esteem, but that remained submissive to God is David.

"When Saul and all Israel heard those words of the Philistine, they were dismayed, and greatly afraid. And David spake to the men that stood by him, saying, What shall be done to the man that killeth this Philistine, and taketh away the reproach from Israel? For who is this uncircumcised Philistine, that he should defy the armies of the living God? David said moreover, The Lord that delivered me out of the paw of the lion, and out of the paw of the Bear, he will deliver me out of the hand of this Philistine. And Saul said unto David, God, and the Lord be with thee."

(1 Samuel 17:11,26-37)

The character displayed by David in his early years is a model of godly self-esteem.

- David displayed knowledge on a subject before using godly wisdom to ascertain his next move.

- Once David perceived the problem at hand and what was at stake, he (knowing who he was in Christ and the power of God) realized that the fight with the Philistine was a battle already won by God.

- David was not intimidated by other fear or disbelief of God's power to win the victory. Often people allow the size or scope of a problem to block the view of their faith in God. This is a sure sign of low self-esteem of who you are and what you are capable of in Christ.

- David's self-esteem in God spilled over onto Saul and caused him to believe that David might pull it off because of his faith in God and his testimony. Self-esteem in a godly person can make others around them better and help set their eyes on what God can do when asked and believed in. David's self-esteem not only gave vision and victory to God's people but gave them a fresh sense of who they were to and in God. Every child of God has the capability to be another David for the Kingdom of God. You must learn and walk in the identity God has revealed to you. A final lesson we learn from David is never to become arrogant or disrespectful to those over or around you who just have not or will not get right with God. *"And he said unto his men, The Lord forbid that I should do this thing [kill Saul] unto my master, the seeing he is the anointed of the Lord, Lord's anointed, to stretch forth mine hand against him."* (1 Samuel 24:6)

Son or daughter of God, I know many problems exist in the church from the pews to the pulpits, but never become so shortsighted that you forget God is in control and God made all people. Do not be a mumbler or backbiter of the people who may be causing problems. For we know it is the spirit behind the people who is the source of the trouble. Do not be fooled into fighting the puppet. Go after the puppet master, Satan. Be a difference-maker because you are called and are equipped with God's power and authority.

CHAPTER 6
Rope Bearers

Is there somebody to teach me? Is there someone to share my joy and pain with? Is there anyone in my life capable of pulling me through when I've given up? Give me vision Lord. Give me a friend.

Have you ever said these words? They are common statements of most Christians. Throughout life we often find ourselves in circumstances that the world finds disdain for. Poverty, incarceration, illiteracy, divorce, or even a sullied reputation are examples of some of life's hard circumstances. You have been dealt a hand that no matter whether you play or deny it, it engulfs and affects you daily. I tell you this day: God's ways are higher than your ways and his thoughts higher than your thoughts.

No matter how low you seem to be or far from respectable you seem to your peers or society, God has a plan and help for you. The hands that work for God are ones that appear with an appearance of favor, or heavenly aristocracy. The Bible says we should not judge by appearances but instead make righteous judgment. This means let the *Word of God* be the judge and plumbline we use to determine matters.

People are often left poor, destitute, and hopeless because the hands that God was working through as rope bearers were dismissed because they did not fit the specifications of the one in need. Wake up to the reality after Adam and Eve, we were all born into a sinful world. The only hands that are clean enough to make our hands fit for God's use and fellowship are Jesus'. Jesus uses the hands of his people still today. God can use anything in this world for our good. A rope bearer can either serve God or Satan. If you are too picky about which hands God helps you with, then Satan has not helped you get close enough to hell yet. Sometimes the hands that seem cultured and firm are the ones that will drop you. The hands God uses may not necessarily pass the eye test, but that is only because they are worn from helping so many before you.

"And Joshua the son of Nun sent out of Shittim two men to spy secretly, saying, Go view the land, even

Jericho. And they went, and came into a harlot's house,

named Rehab, and lodged there." (Joshua 2:1)

In this scripture, we have two men sent to spy on the land for God's people. The first-time spies were sent to search out the land, only two came back with a good report. Because of this, the people did not believe the land could be taken by them, disbelieved God's word through Moses, and were sentenced by God to die in the wilderness (see Numbers 14). Now, after forty years of roaming in the desert, God chose to allow the Israelites into the promised land. As Joshua sent out the spies, can you imagine the burden these two men carried on their backs?

Notice the similarities between your life and this story. Man, think of the times God has sent you to do something after putting you through something. God may have tried to move in your life through people asking you to Sunday school but once they grew weary of chasing you down, you stopped going. God may have allowed you to be exposed to Christians to give you positive examples to follow Him, but you found them boring and soon alienated or removed yourself from them. God may even have allowed you to have a run-in with police or be incarcerated to get your focus on Him, but you never sought Him once the trouble passed or you were released.

Israel is just like us and we are like Israel. God chastises until we get it right. Some people never get it right and do not put their trust in God, so they eventually die in their sin serving Satan. We all need help to do God's will. Our ultimate help is always from God, but how and who God uses to deliver us is God's business.

"Then she let them down by a cord [rope] through the window; for her house was upon the town wall, and she dwelt upon the wall." (Joshua 2:15)

A harlot was whom God entrusted the spies of His nation to. This was no mere chance that the woman's house was located on the wall. God knew that although she was practicing immoral sins for a time, her heart would respond to his desire to use her.

Some readers may need a set of circumstances to be their rope bearer so they can in turn be a rope bearer to God's people. Once a man or woman realizes God's true desire for them, there is an opportunity to respond with zealous submission and servitude towards God and others. Up to the very moment Rahab was called upon to be a rope bearer, the people around her thought all she would ever be a harlot.

If you are not yet a believer, consider this? What if what you have heard about the God of Israel is true? What if He really can deliver you from a meaningless existence into an intimate fellowship with Him? You have never heard of a God who speaks to His people in a voice from a mountain top, but if there is a God like this, would you let Him use you how He wanted? You have let everyone else use you like they wanted and did not even get satisfaction or thanks.

Pray this prayer: God of Israel! If you are real send someone who represents you to help me get to know you. If you do, I will serve you the rest of my life. No more drugs, no more stripping, no more... well...no more serving other gods.

God has people in churches, governments, and various other places that have the capabilities and callings to be rope bearers to others but because of people's lack of faith in God to change, clean, and use anyone--these rope bearers remain unused. You must stop looking at the circumstances and identities people have masqueraded as or hid behind outside of Christ.

When anyone comes to Christ, they are a new creature and have a new heart. Their outer appearance may not change, but because Jesus Christ is now their foundation of strength, they have limitless capabilities. Many people that consider only the outer appearance of an individual to decide if they could be a rope bearer for God will realize at some point that they missed a blessing simply because of their lack of faith in God being able to use people to help them.

"Therefore, the princes said unto the king, we beseech thee, let this man [Jeremiah] be put to death. Then took they Jeremiah and cast him into the dungeon of Malchiah the son of Hammelech, that was in the court of the prison: and they let down Jeremiah

with cords. And in the dungeon, there was no water, but mire: so Jeremiah sunk in the mire." (Jeremiah 38:4,6)

See how the nobility of Jeremiah's time are the ones casting him into the dungeon. There are rope bearers of Satan that exist also. These are individuals sent into your life to drop you down to the pits of hell. Satan is not ignorant to what you like and dislike. Most of the time when you are trying to serve God out of a carnal mind and luke-warm dedication, Satan sends people that look good, sound good, and even persuade you to do some good things.

The princes of Jeremiah's time represent the respect and accolades we crave from the world today. The approval and power we crave to be granted success as society defines it. Everyday people come into Christians' lives to try to shake their faith and create division in their purpose. Satan does not offer you only things such as a glance from a married woman or temptation to steal from the workplace. He knows that some will fall to these small temptations but a believer in Christ that is walking close to God will easily dismiss these temptations. Beware, Satan sends worldly friends to involve you through acts of omission or commission to approve their wrongdoing.

These are some of Satan's princes that he uses to drag you slowly but methodically into decisions and a lifestyle that can lead to hell. Throughout the Bible and even today, there are people who should be a rope bearer for Christ but are bearing Satan's ropes instead. They have a tight grip, so you are not lowered too fast but once you hit bottom, they release the rope.

I am not saying that all people that appear good are not. I am saying that many Christian communities that are blessed with rope bearers are lost because they are asking for the wrong signs to identify a godly rope bearer. Love, peace, patience, and salvation are trademarks of God's rope bearers. For though a person may be kind, powerful, and giving, without Jesus as Lord they are depending on self and operate through limited strength to bear your rope. Humans grow weary through their own weaknesses, but God's strength operating in their lives makes them strong in their weakness.

In Luke's parable (Luke 10:25-37), two men look the part of God's people but act the part of Satan's. Stop looking at who you think God can or will use to help your infirmities and by faith ask God to send you someone who will. Titles such as government or church do not guarantee that someone is sent by God to help you. Jesus came not with a title, but a God ordained purpose.

God's rope bearers will be purposeful towards businessmen, farmers, teenagers, as well as backsliders', murderers, and prostitutes. Many shepherds throughout the **Bible** are all men who God has used to be rope bearers to a nation. I am also not saying you must be a person with a suspect background to be a rope bearer. I am saying the problem has never been accepting help from men such as Samuel who have a spotless record and background, but from men like Moses who was a murderer and Peter who was a liar.

A person at times is called to spiritually be a rope bearer used by the Holy Spirit to help a specific people or an individual. An example of this is Daniel. This man was a Hebrew of unusual humility. Humility is a pleasing thing before God, for He sees pride as an abomination. Daniel is not only highlighted as an example of humility for Christians, but also as an example of a spiritual rope bearer of God's people.

"Now when Daniel knew that the writing was signed, he went into his house; and his windows being open in his chamber, toward Jerusalem, he kneeled upon his knees three times a day, and prayed, and gave thanks before his God, as he did aforetime." (Daniel 6:10)

Daniel was faced with a death sentence if he petitioned any god or man for thirty days. Still, prayed to his God as he routinely had done for quite some time. Daniel refused to be removed from his position of a rope bearer for God's people.

Rope bearers must be consistent in exercising spiritual disciplines such as prayer, fasting, and fellowship in their relationship with God! You cannot be a constant source of strength or rescue for your brothers or your sisters in Christ if you are easily swayed by emotions and situations. Emotions influence us in many ways, but when you allow emotions to dictate your behavior as a Christian rather than the Holy Spirit, you become an unstable rope bearer. Throughout your days of pulling others through and above situations, Satan will try to make you let go of the rope that is a lifeline to others.

We as God's rope bearers are the salt of the earth. If we lose our saltiness we will be trodden over. You must stand for others through your witness daily. Satan is not scared if only in your private life you are a powerful rope bearer of God. Satan is exposed and his works destroyed when your skills, gifts, and witness make up the cords of rescue for others.

"And when he [King Darius] came to the den, he cried with a lamentable voice unto Daniel; and the king spake and said to Daniel, 0 Daniel, servant of the living God, is the God, whom thou servest continually, able to deliver thee from the lions? Then said Daniel unto the king, O king, live forever." (Daniel 6:20-21)

Daniel's witness was so powerful that after King Darius had thrown him in the lion's den, the king ran down early the next morning and cried to Daniel, "Did God deliver you?"

Daniel not only answered yes but greeted the king with a salutation that King Darius should live forever. This is a rope bearing witness. The King immediately had Daniel hoisted out of the den of lions. The men and their families who schemed to have this done to Daniel were thrown into the lion's den and a proclamation was made to fear and tremble before the true God of Daniel.

Stop making excuses on your job, in your spare time, and at church for your witness not being a good one. Many people fail to realize that by being a good witness for God, He will use your witness to pull others out of the snares of Satan.

The Bible says, "For the children of this world are in their generation wiser than the children of light." (Luke 16:8)

What!? Satan's kids are smarter than us? How? Well, the drug dealers flash promises of quick money and extravagant living without toil or wait. The psychics promise glimpses into the future to appease doubts and guarantee destinies. Some apostate ministers, laypeople, and others in our church preach the message with no anointing or conviction and instead promise the blessings of God will come with good attendance, reading your Bible, and praying. (Please note: Attending church, reading the Word, and praying are all an important part of a Christian's walk with God but trials, salvation, and being led by the Holy Spirit are some unseen and un-preached things that must go hand and hand with these.)

Satan is influencing our world through pictures, movies, and music while captivating minds with hell originated ideas. Get up off your hypocritical ideas and self-aggrandizing dreams and be a rope bearer like Daniel. Go through things and still smile. Do not say a lot but do what glorifies God. Some people need to see a Christian's walk before they will go hear a sermon.

Many come to Christ focusing on self and are scared to fall and look bad before others. A rope bearer that has been seasoned in faith and experienced enough to go in the pit and not look downcast is the rope bearer we all need. Daniel's purpose was to be a witness to the power of God through his work for God. We all are equipped with gifts of the Holy Spirit to edify the body of Christ (see Romans 12, 1 Corinthians 12, and Ephesians 4). Seek God's face and ask Him to reveal your purpose as a rope bearer.

The only prerequisite is that you must be in a relationship with God through Jesus Christ. You cannot edify a spiritual body that you are not even a part of. I am not saying God does not use unsaved people to help the church. I am saying a rope bearer's work is God's work and only what is of God will withstand. So, if you are unsaved and helping the church, you are not a rope bearer but just an individual who is living for Satan but being used by God (see Proverbs 16:4).

You must not depend on others to always be a rope bearer for you. There are times when others cannot see, and you must not only be the rope bearer God uses but also be the visionary that gets it straight from the Lord. Ask yourself: How any times have I taken the lead on a project God has told me too? You cannot just think about edifying yourself but also the body. Sometimes you will be at the edge of your wits and efforts which can cause a condition some call anxiety or worry. In the case of a rope bearer of God, this is called, "climb time."

Climb time can be a time to evaluate your faith and position through Christ to help others in different circumstances. It can also be a time to tighten your grip on the unseen and appropriate God's Word to move from the seen to the unseen reality of miracles. Throughout your life you have been in predicaments, and you will face more predicaments where you must climb to grow.

Most climbers use the same ropes to pull one another up, climb, and ensure safety. This same system applies in the life of Christians. The same experiences that you had to go through and be pulled out of will help you pull someone else up. The Bible is a rope that calls all Christians out of the valleys in our lives. There is no other help. The Word of God is a lasso around our spirituality that tells us when to pull and when to be drawn up and beyond the mountains of life.

Sometimes churches do not meet the needs of their people because they try to say so much about subjects that do not even seem to be relevant to the congregation's weekly struggles. Never forget that though we are spiritual people, we still must reach people where they are at. Jesus, being God manifested in the flesh, held all power and dominion of the Holy Ghost. He never spoke or did things that went over the heads of the people He was helping.

Today many of our churches have become so influenced by the world that we have forgotten that a true man of God bares a rope for leading and discipling. Church elders want a minister who is skilled enough to feed yet entertain them; a counselor who will seek the face of God like Moses but go along with them when the answer does not fit their agenda.

Jesus was a lamb and a lion. He carried a staff and a rod. He loved but did not waver in speaking God's Word. We are being in the express image of God are just like Jesus. We must stop pacifying sin because of our embarrassment of it being exposed. We must stop telling the preachers and prophets of God not to preach or proclaim something because of the stronghold of deceitfulness in the hearts of many church goers.

We must also be wary of messages from the church that God only manifests or works in a certain way. If God did it before, He can do it again if He so desires. Indeed. No man knows the full mind of God and this being so, each of us bares a responsibility to discipline one another with sound doctrine and love. We are the express image of God, so let us have the mind and actions of Christ. Be a voice and prayer warrior of God to the people. You may not physically carry a wooden cross on your back and be bloody, but you can carry the burdens of the body of Christ to God for others and feel the pain of others by spiritually bridging the gap.

In Luke 7:25 Jesus asked the people, *"But what went ye out for to see? A man clothed in soft raiment? Behold, they which are gorgeously appareled, and live delicately, are in king's courts."*

Jesus was speaking about John the Baptist. His point was that the people went to hear the voice of God through John, but when they were taken aback not just by the power of God in John but by his accusations and uncovering of sins. Don't you know that God is not playing with you when He speaks to you? Whether it be in a small 50-year-old church in Freeport, Illinois, or a sprawling church in Houston, Texas, God is not playing with you.

When you go to church do not expect your titles, suits, and good deeds to hide you from the piercing Word of God. Maybe you attend church in casual apparel thinking that God is a friend like a bar buddy or a co-worker. God is God and must be respected as such. He came down from heaven and took the form of Jesus Christ. He suffered as a man but was perfectly loving and daily God.

Examine yourself today. If every sermon you hear is sweet sounding to your ears, then I ask: How is this truly the voice of God? The Bible says God's Word is "sharper than any two-edged sword." What sword that is sharp does not cut?

Rope bearers, I call you to arms in the name of Jesus. Stop accepting every rope you are given for help. The Bible says that Satan will come as an angel of light sometimes. Do not rescue me and others with ropes intertwined with condescending attitudes, secret ungodly motives, or pride. Help people with the rough ropes braided of righteousness, the coarse knots of discipline, and infinite strands of love.

There can be people who attend church regularly but have not allowed the church to be in them. In other words, these individuals have a Savior in Christ, not a Lord. A Lord gives commands, understands his people, and is given reverence. People get mad when a strong rebuke comes from the pulpit or the church but understand that Satan is the one who pacifies sin – NOT GOD. So, stop expecting to get helped with a pat on the back and a hug when you know, and God knows that a slap on the bottom and intensive chastising is what may be needed.

When I began writing this book, I thought that many people would not like it because of its directness but I also know that the power of God spoken in truth can change lives. The power of God is operating as you read this book. This book is a rope not to make people happy or sad, but to bring remembrance of God's Word as well as the conviction and exhortations of the Holy Spirit. Jesus, John, and many others of God's rope bearers' words were insulting to the ears and acted as a wrecking ball on the lies of Satan's kingdom but because of the power of God these same words brought change and life to people of God.

Do not be a rope bearer in name and reputations alone – but in power as 1 Corinthians 4:20 says, *"For the kingdom of God is not in speech but in power."* Despite popular opinion in church, the Word of

God says many ways you have got to go through something God's way to become God's vessel of honor. After you have been blessed, accept the salvation of the Lord, and dedicate your every activity to climbing and dropping ropes of God. The kingdom of God is constantly being built and molded to God's image of it.

Joseph's life demonstrated a rope bearer's mentality, purpose, and legacy but was rooted in humble beginnings.

"And Joseph was brought down to Egypt, and Potiphar an officer of Pharaoh captain of the guard, an Egyptian, bought him out of the hand of the Ishmaelites, which had brought him down thither. And Joseph's master took him, and put into the prison, a place where the king's prisoners were bound; and he was there in prison." (Genesis 39:1, 20)

A rope bearer will find themselves in situations orchestrated by God for the purpose of them helping others. Joseph was sold into slavery by his brothers and put in prison by a master he faithfully served. The master's wife lied about him. God allowed all of this.

Realize today rope bearers, your circumstances do not always reflect your true behavior, nor are they easily understood (see Proverbs 3:56). Joseph was innocent of wrongdoing in these matters, yet he was abused and punished. This happened to him for God's purposes. He was allowed to fall into these situations.

Therefore perseverance is necessary for a rope bearer. The working of perseverance brings about patience and many other good things of God. Do not be afraid of the consequences of being a rope bearer for the intrinsic good is everlasting and the circumstantial bad is only momentary. Stand strong in the fact that God will never leave or forsake you. Do not try to figure out the why's of everything, but instead seek the lessons.

"And there was with us a young man, a Hebrew, servant to the captain of the quad; and we told him, and he interpreted to us our dreams; to man according to his dream he did interpret. And Pharaoh said unto Joseph: "For as much as God hath showed thee all this, there is none as discreet and wise as thou art." (Genesis 41:12, 39)

Joseph was where God wanted him to be. Him using the gift of interpreting dreams that God gave him in addition to being a good rope bearer even when he was falsely accused and abused, allowed God to work in others' lives.

You may have experienced years of misery, loneliness, or other bad experiences. You need to know that God is over all things. It does not matter if you liked the experiences or believe they were from God (see Romans 8:28). God set you up to be at this point in your life. You did not understand it at the time, but God had a purpose for everything you have gone through. Stop living haunted by questions of how and why and do God's work with fervency and vision knowing that God is a rewarder of him who diligently seeks Him. He feels the pain of losses and bad breaks, but God wants you to understand that He needed you right where you were. God created you just for the unique life and purpose you are living out. If someone else could do it, they would have. You have been chosen!

A rope bearer understands that God is always in control and works continually to do God's will knowing it is not in vain (see 2 Corinthians 7:9-12). God allows sorrow to bring about a more excellent work in you. Empathy is talked about, but it seems no one wants to live a life to be qualified to intimately and experientially minister to others out of it. Jesus did and no servant is greater than his master. Have not the lost loves, pain of letting go, and other sorrowful experiences driven you to seek comfort in the Lord? Continue to abide in Christ and you shall bear fruit as Joseph did. The trials of a Christian will always yield a blessing for the future.

"And God sent me before you to preserve your posterity in the earth, and to save your lives by a great deliverance. So now it was not you that sent me hither, but God; and he hath made me a father to Pharaoh, and of his entire house, and a ruler throughout the land of Egypt." (Genesis 45:7-8)

Just as Joseph was not allowed to be placed in circumstances and experience them just for himself - neither are you. Rope bearer, you must not only obtain your blessings, but blessings for others too. The true essence of a blessing is allowing it to bless others also. This is loving your neighbor as yourself. You may not own what I own, but I can help you with the things I own. You may not fast and pray and hear God's voice as I do, but I can be a intercessor for you in these ways. A rope bearer knows that to be blessed you must bless. We are many parts, but one body. Your efficiency or deficiency affects me. I thank God because I know inside each of you who have accepted Jesus Christ is the Holy Spirit, which is also in me, and *"we can do all things through Christ Jesus."* (Philippians 4:13) Ropebearer rise and raise those beside you; with you.

"And Joseph said unto them, Fear not: for am I in the place of God? But as for you, ye thought evil against me; but God meant it unto good, to bring to pass, as it is this day, to save much people alive." (Genesis 50:19-20)

This was not a declaration of Joseph that it was ok for his brothers to have done him so harshly. This *was* a providential imparting of God's mercy on these men. These were to be the fathers of the tribes of Israel.

Every man (including me) and woman reading this book has wronged someone. Whether it was in thought or deed matters not. For sin is sin before God. God is saying that we are all forgiven if we will just confess, repent, and call on the name of Jesus as our Lord and Savior. Joseph's brothers have been living in Egypt with Joseph over them. The past sins they had done to him lingered in their minds. Are you at the point in your life where you are haunted by past sins you committed (possibly against others)? What if so and so has not forgiven me? How can I show love when I did such and such to them?

My haunted rope bearer, confess and believe God has forgiven you. People may hold you accountable with guilt, but God does not. Your guilt will not change one bit of the consequences for your sin, but your confessing, living guilt free, and moving on will. Whether you wait twenty seconds or twenty years to confess and repent, God will forgive you and accept you. He will shed light on the lie of Satan that the worse the sin, the longer you should feel guilty. The only thing God looks at is the sincerity and willingness for your confession and repentance - not the length of time you felt was sufficient to suffer before giving it to God.

Do not be like Joseph's brothers. They had access to all the forgiveness and blessings of God, all those years. On the outside they enjoyed, but inside they were fearful. Be free, in the name of Jesus, from self-imposed guilt and exile. Be loosed from the guilt others try to keep you oppressed by. *"If the Son [Jesus] therefore shall make you free, ye shall be free indeed."* (John 8:36)

Enjoy the freedom found in Christ. You cannot change the past, but you can allow others and self to use those experiences as steppingstones to make difference for God.

CHAPTER 7
Walking Comfortably (In the Anointing)

This chapter was crucial to my development as a mature Christian. So many people seek the anointing of God in their lives. However, they do not take the time to realize that just as a 6'9", 18-year-old boy must become acquainted with the height he recently obtained or a pregnant woman must learn to function with the quickly added weight gain, an individual truly blessed with the anointing of God must learn to function, submit, and see this awesome power of God for His glory.

I have never met a new Christian that does not want to live out the promises of God, share their newly found faith, and walk over Satan just as Jesus did.

"Go ye therefore, and teach all nations, baptizing them in the name of the Father, and of the Son, and of the Holy Ghost: teaching them to observe all things whatsoever I have commanded you: and, lo I am with you always, even unto the end of the world. Amen." (Matthew 28:19-20)

"And he said unto them, go ye into all the world, and preach the gospel to every creature. He that

believeth and is baptized shall be saved; but he that believeth not shall be damned. And these signs shall follow them that believe; In my name shall they cast out devils; they shall speak with new tongues; They shall take up serpents; and if they drink any deadly thing, it shall not hurt them; they shall lay hands on the sick, and they shall recover." (Mark16:15-18)

These are all things a Christian can do. One thing people realize after the inception of their walk with God is the reality of what Peter told early Christians, *"Beloved, think it not strange concerning the fiery trial, which is to try you, as though some strange thing happened unto you: but rejoice, inasmuch as ye are partakers of Christ's sufferings.; that when his glory shall be revealed, ye may be glad also with exceeding joy."* (1 Peter 4:12-13)

A newly converted Christian or one who has been a Christian but desires nothing more than salvation and blessings are taught to reverence God and be aware of His power by being tried in fire of experience. These men or women want the anointing and authority of Christ in their lives to do all the Bible says they can, but often forget every rainbow is preceded by a storm.

Yes, upon acceptance of Christ as Lord and Savior you have the power to overcome and send Satan packing, but without the peace and knowledge of what to do with it – you are a lean mean fighting machine that does not recognize your enemy. Satan's tactics can leave you confused and doubting. People who get saved are typically told they can do all things through Christ who strengthens them and go out to fight Satan with the courage of a lion. Nobody tells them Satan is going to fight back with defamation of character, depression, loneliness, and even use the children to get to them. To truly be comfortable in the anointing of Christ you must wait on and be led by the Holy Spirit.

"And being assembled together with them, commanded them [Jesus did] that they should not depart from Jerusalem, but wait for the promise of the Father, which, saith he, ye have of heard of me. But ye shall receive power, after that the Holy Ghost is come upon you: and ye shall be witnesses unto me both in Jerusalem of Judea, and in Samaria, and unto the uttermost parts of the earth." (Acts I:4, 8)

The blueprint of learning to walk comfortable in the anointing of God is to pray, wait on the Holy Spirit to empower you, and move in obedience and love as the Holy Spirit leads. I cannot tell you when every aspect of baptism of the Holy Spirit takes place. I can say that God's Word says God will give us the things we request of Him in Jesus' Name according to His will. Many people will complicate this and other matters. I tell you to seek the face of God and ask Him to teach and lead you on this matter. When you pray, stand on these verses:

"But the Comforter, which is the Holy Ghost, who the Father will send in my name, he shall teach you all things, and bring all things to your remembrance, whatsoever I have said unto you." (John 14:26)

"But the anointing which ye have received of him abideth in you, and ye need not that any man teach you: about the same anointing teacheth you of all things, and is truth, and is no lie, and even as it hath taught you, ye shall abide in him." (1 John 2:27)

Too many people want to tell you what God told them and do not also recommend you consulting God yourself on the matter. God may teach or help you understand this point through other people, but there is no better student of God than the one who submits to God first and invites Him to manifest his lessons through whomever and however He wants. God is the best teacher there is or ever will be!

The anointing breaks yokes and teaches, but many a person these days and in the Bible were overwhelmed and intimidated by the same anointing. God gave and continues to give his anointing so you can overcome Satan, find direction, and understand God's love and purpose for you to help others.

"And when the Lord saw that he turned aside to see, God called unto him out of the midst of the bush,

and said, Moses, Moses. And he said, Here am I:
Come now therefore, and I will send thee unto
Pharaoh, that thou mayest bring forth my people. The
children of Israel out of Egypt. And Moses said to God,
Who am I, that I should go unto Pharaoh and that I
should bring forth the children of Israel out of Egypt."
(Exodus 3:4-11)

Moses was a murderer on the run hiding far from
the land of Egypt. Do you know that no matter how far
you run because of your mistakes or sins, if God has a
plan for you, He will find and cleanse you?

When Moses first sees the burning bush
representing God's presence, he feels confused.
Though the bush was burning it was not consumed by
the flame. The anointing, though powerful and
consuming, will only purify God's people even more.
Moses was witnessing what God was doing to him on

the inside. He did not have an immediate understanding or recognition of this fact, but our knowledge or lack thereof cannot impede God's mercy and a heart willing to serve God.

God's people had been crying for help in escaping the slavery of Egypt. God heard their cries and upon His timing chose and anointed Moses to rescue his people. Moses felt like many of us. We become saved, come into a knowledge of God, and realize we are so far from the perfection and righteousness of God that we want to hide from Him.

This is the sin nature of every human. We were (because of Adam and Eve's sin) separated from God, but praise God for his mercy and Jesus for sacrificing himself for us (see John 3:16). We are reconciled to God because of his choice, mercy, and will.

Before anyone says yes to God, He must say yes to them. No individual can come to claim Jesus as

Lord and Savior unless God draws them (see John 6:44-45). God chose Moses as He chooses us. Though our past sins and inadequacies try to hinder us, we must realize it is the anointing that makes us something Satan and the world fear and recognize. They fear us because of who we represent. They recognize us because we are ministers of life to a dying world.

When people realize it is not about deserving the blessings or degree of anointing God gives us but His mercy and grace, then people will stop thinking they must earn or deserve the anointing. Every individual who serves God will face hard situations and be asked to do things beyond themselves. This is where the anointing of God truly carries them up and over every obstacle and doubt. All of you chose to do mighty things. By putting faith in Jesus Christ, you chose to do mighty things.

Realize that if you could do things alone or overcome them by yourself, you would not need God. Some people claim deliverance over alcohol, lust, and other sins of self but modified is not the same as delivered. Realize God created you to need Him and without having done something through God, Satan is still near in a disguise. Lust becomes anger, alcohol abuse becomes an addition to sports, and so on. Knowing you are limited to accomplish or do anything lasting outside of God should give gravity to the anointing of God.

Moses did not want to go even though he was chosen and anointed by God, but God told Moses his name and promised to work wonders through him to substantiate his godly authority. You too have been given the name Jesus to glorify God. This is insignificant to the world but to the anointed of God it is power. Just go into churches and streets and begin to proclaim Jesus, Jesus, Jesus and see the responses you get. People either want to run from you or hear what you are going to say next. There is power in that name.

God told Moses He would perform miracles through him and then gave Moses' revelation through the proclamation that God's name was, "I am that I am." Jesus said you and I can and will do many miracles in his name. To truly know the power of the anointing, you must boldly proclaim Jesus' name and always give Him the glory. Do not think your power is in eloquent speech or worldly wisdom. Accept and glory in the fact that it is only through Jesus Christ you can do all things.

Even after knowing the power in the anointing of Lord, some still have problems being comfortable in it. Isaiah was a man such as this. Isaiah's name means "God is salvation." This man knew God intimately and served him faithfully but when it came time for him to walk in the anointing of a specific ministry, he was as a child (see Isaiah 6:5).

Isaiah, though a man of God, realized that in the presence of God he was filthy with his own sin and was burdened because he dwelt among filthy conversations of the people (see 1 Corinthians 15:33). God knows right where each of his children are in their walks with Him. Nothing that you are surrounded by, have seen, or done can subvert God's grace. None of it takes God by surprise.

I know from experience that when God calls you to begin specific ministry or kingdom work, the first thing you do is look in the mirror and say, "Who am I when I have done so much wrong? How can God use me? I don't want to go. The tendency is to try to recoil from the voice of God and stay in a mode of stagnancy. We all do it but some to a greater degree than others. The disciples did it in Acts. If you read the first six chapters of Acts, you see the power of God moving and blessing, but nobody is going to witness anywhere. Then God allowed some dissension and persecution to happen to get his commandments obeyed.

When Jesus said the disciples would be empowered, he also told them to go throughout the world and proclaim the gospel. The disciples had forgotten the anointing was to be used to further the kingdom and not just share among one another. How many of you only associate with Christians? Though the Bible says do not be friends with the world, you are still no better than Jesus. Become servants and proclaimers of the gospel of Jesus Christ.

Many a night I cried, prayed, and fasted for more anointing, but God showed me I just needed to become more adept in using what He had a ready given me. I was seeking righteousness so much that I became like the disciples--stagnant. I felt like Isaiah in rewards to sin. The Holy Spirit helped me realize that there has been only one sinless person, Jesus Christ.

Once this truth soaked into me, I slowly through the Holy Spirit became comfortable with the fact that who Jesus Christ has set free is free indeed. God knows my past and present and has cleansed and used me. God has called me righteous, His, and more than a conqueror. It matters not what mother, father, society, or Satan tries to call me or make me believe I am. Simply, I am who God calls me and since his Word is everlasting, I choose to be a son of the king.

The problem has never been race or affluence when it comes anointing. Throughout the Bible black, white, brown, slave, king, Jew, and Gentile have died to self and accepted and believed in Christ. They all learned that the anointing is their hope and joy.

Today, some people are told they are good and do not need God to approve them or that because even though they are not perfect, trying hard would be enough to get them into heaven. These are lies and I denounce them in Jesus' name. The skeptic or deceiver who's reading this book may think I am judging or making rash statements, but I ask you to look to the Bible. The men who the Bible calls righteous such as Jesus, Moses, David, and Peter, have outlasted men such as Korah, Ahithophel, the zealots, and Caiaphas in reputation, notoriety, and honor. These men of ancient times who were enemies of God's servants and enjoyed power and dictated what was acceptable to nations are not even recognizable to most people of the world today. They were good in the eyes of the majority but to God they were enemies. Good outside of God does not exist and is not respected by God. Only what is of God will stand and be honored in the kingdom of heaven. The anointing of

God is the only thing that will keep you on judgment day.

So how did Isaiah evolve from an insecure man of God into a more precise and action filled anointing? He didn't! God did it for him!

"Then flew one of the seraphim unto me, having a live coal in his hand. Which he had taken with the tongs from off the altar: end he laid it upon my mouths and said, Lo, this hath touched thy lips: and thine iniquity is taken away, and thy, sin purged. Also I heard the voice of the Lord, saying:"Whom shall I send, and who will go for us? "Then said I, Here am I send me." (Isaiah 6:6-8)

Isaiah was undone at first when the Lord spoke to him through the angel. Then, after being cleansed, was bold and zealous to do God's work. So many men's and women's lives are testimonies to the cleansing power of God. There is something about God's forgiveness and mercy regarding our sin that makes us want to go serve Him more wholeheartedly. The weight of sin cannot be measured in pounds, but in amount of difficulty and hardship it causes. A person must realize that daily in a Christian's walk there must be confession and forsaking of sin. No matter how many years or days you have been a Christian, you must walk in the understanding that only God can cleanse and renew you from sin and its negative effects. Being comfortable in confessing sin to God and allowing Him to keep working in your mind concerning sin releases you from the weight of failure or vanity in trying to make your walk perfect. This is not an excuse to sin. This is a truth you can only overcome by daily walking by the Spirit and abiding in Christ.

After personally experiencing this, I began to walk as God would have me walk. I still sin, but the frequency and motives of the sins are things I seek to defeat daily even as I am maturing in my walk. Do not grow weary seeking righteousness and perfection in Christ and never forget they are gifts of God.

Isaiah could do no more than be willing to acknowledge his wrongs, ask God to forgive him, and ask God to use him. People complicate God. Walking comfortably in the anointing is far more than trying to stop sinning, it is surrendering and realizing God is faithful, will forgive your sins, and use you. We always must work for God as if everything depends upon us while knowing full well that everything we do depends upon God.

The anointed of God will intimidate man. People fail to realize that when God calls and confirms an individual's calling, all that person must do is submit to and obey God. So many, including myself, try to figure out how we can do what God has placed in our hearts and given us vision to do but we can only do these things as the Holy Spirit shows us how and when. Trust and obedience are the keys to accepting the call and doing the work God equipped you to do (see Proverbs 3:5-6).

Even knowing this, the call can be challenging and leave us feeling disoriented at times. Joshua experienced this himself.

"And it came to pass, when Joshua was by Jericho that he lifted up his eyes and looked, and behold there stood a man over against him with his sword drawn in his hand: and Joshua went unto him, and said unto him, Art thou for us, or for our adversaries? And He said, Nay, but as captain of the host of the Lord am I now come." (Joshua 5:13-14)

Joshua had just been filled with a spirit of wisdom by the laying on of hands by Moses in Deuteronomy 34:9. He had been told by God *that "no man would be able to stand before thee all the days of thy life,"* in Joshua 1:5. Even with this wisdom and promise of God, Joshua proceeded to be intimidated by a man of large stature with a sword. It is amazing how we can believe so much in the power of God, walk in the anointing of God, and still lose focus. Along with this wisdom and promise came pressure to lead as Moses led and command a people to obtain the Promised Land.

Men and women in churches across the world are anointed by the Holy Spirit to do the work God calls them to do but suddenly they let the reality of this world become more vivid than God in their minds. Joshua knew he was called and anointed to do the work but the man with a drawn sword caused his vision (peripheral and spiritual) to be drawn to only what he could see.

How many men come out of their prayer closets having just received revelation and confirmation from God about their lives only to in the next few minutes lose track of the vision and instructions God gave because of something like a phone call that seemingly contradicts the spiritual answers he just received? Realize that it is what God says it is, not what circumstances or people say it is. When Jesus died on the cross, people said it was a victory against Christians, but it was victory for Christians. When David sinned against God with Bathsheba people said it was unpardonable, but God allowed David's first son to die because of the sin and the second (Solomon) to live and prosper because of David's repentance.

Stop letting Satan rob you of walking in the authority of the anointing. God is God. Romans 8:28

says, "All things work together for good to them that love God, to them who are the called according to his purpose." This speaks directly to Christians. It is saying that we cannot worry about what seems to be difficult or but to remember God is our Father and He does not seek to confound or confuse us. Satan daily throws perspectives of reality at us to dissuade and distract but rely on godly faith and vision to accomplish God's work. In Jesus' name, go forth standing on God's Word and walking in the power of God.

Slogans, gimmicks, and philosophies will get our bottoms kicked by Satan. Neat encouragements like "take one step and God will take the other" or "don't worry about it because none of us is perfect" can be true statements, but they can also be excuses. We as the body of Christ must move on to greater things. We must stop justifying sin and accepting mediocrity from the pulpits, choirs, and congregations. Just because some Christians are carnal and lukewarm is no excuse for you to be.

Throughout the Bible, God took the few and did miracles. You who are sold out to God are the few. Note that they did not have degrees behind their name, boast about the size of their church, or brag about the awards received for doing God's work. God does not recognize these things if they are not for his glory and according to his will. Christianity has descended so far into lukewarmness that a Christian being what a Christian is supposed to be is not always seen as such.

"But which of you, having a servant plowing or feeding cattle, will say unto him, by and by, when he is come from the field, Go and sit down to meat? And will not rather say unto him, make ready wherewith I may sup, and gird thyself, and serve me, till I have eaten and drunken; and afterward thou shalt eat and drink?

Doth, he thank that servant because he did the things that were commanded him? I think not. So likewise, ye, when ye shall have done all those things which are commanded, say, We are unprofitable servants: we have done that which was our duty to do." (Luke 17:7-10)

We are sons and daughter of God, saints holy and righteous in end through Jesus Christ, but we are servants to God first. You cannot worship God without salvation, and you obtain salvation to be saved from hell and to praise God.

We (the church) have lost focus. It is to the point that in most churches if a man stood up and wanted to be saved, he would be out of order for not waiting until the altar call. Is it by conformity to man's agenda that people only get saved at the end of most church services or is it coincidence?

To those of you who think their church is not like that, when is the last time someone stood up during the middle of church and got saved? For churches walking in the anointing of God and seeing these souls saved throughout service, why are you not testifying and encouraging this in other services? Raise your expectations for self and for the church.

Everybody wants to be blessed, but most people do not believe it can happen as illustrated by 2 Kings 7:19, *"And that lord answered the man of God, and said, now, behold if the Lord should make windows in heaven, might such a thing be? And he said, Behold, thou shalt see it with thine eyes, but shalt not eat thereof."*

Because of disbelief, many a person has missed the joy and peace found in Jesus Christ. To use a common example, consider blind dates. These happen daily with the hopes of having fun, but most single Christians want more than fun. They want a lasting relationship with the mate God has chosen for them. Most people do not go into blind dates with the idea this could be their future husband or wife. Why? Because they do not believe that one lunch or talk could lead to a lifetime of happiness. So, instead they meander through life hoping the quantity of blind dates will yield a prosperous and godly find.

Once a Christian thinks in their heart even for just a moment that something is impossible or too big for God, they have said God is too small to handle his own creation. It sounds absurd, but millions live life on this principle today. Learn your potential in Philippians 4:13, God's expectations for you in Mark 16:15-18, and realize that Matthew 6:33 and 5:6 can and will be your way of life through Jesus Christ as your Lord and Savior.

Walking comfortably in the anointing takes humility, not false modesty. Today some Christians are highly anointed but have allowed Satan to shackle them with a fear that has actually deceived them concerning who God has blessed them to be. How many times have you known in your heart that God gave you the love, wisdom, and talent to do some project only to be silent because you were afraid of the responsibility that would come forth with the project? How many times have you helped behind the scenes because you are scared? No more than a light can be hidden in a dark cave than the anointing of wisdom, leadership, or whatever be hidden in you. Do not fear saying, "I'm anointed to do this." This fear is not of God!

When you go to a restaurant and they bring you the wrong order, you tell them so. Why can't we tell people what expectations we have for our churches, children, and lives? People are scared to speak boldly when the anointing stirs them because of their own sin or timidity in speaking words or life. The preachers preach despair, problems, and donations. The mothers speak sadness at the plight of their children. Single men speak whoredom concerning anything that moves--some are even so lost they crave men.

This day, realize God shows you problems to pray down not tear down. Mothers, begin to claim salvation and peace in your children's lives and do not watch them more than you watch God. As you watch and obey God, He will rescue, teach, and mature your children.

Ministers, stop using the pulpit for personal agendas of politics, gossip, and causes. Your number one cause is to preach Jesus. When you preach God's Word it will lead people to do the things you are trying to get them to do. Jesus preached the kingdom of heaven and obedience knowing social reform, financial responsibilities, and morality reforms would follow.

Single men, ask God to change your pleasures to godly ones, your conquests into souls for Christ, and your boasting of freedom into dynamic spirit led liberty that produces revival everywhere.

For a rebirth to take place the space must become too small or obsolete for the existence of the living thing. Growth is similar. To grow is to become more than what you once were. The thing that is most painful is the toil that comes with growth. The birth of a child, the birth of an animal, and the realizing of potential and walking in it are not easy processes. All three are followed by a life that touches more than themselves. One child's birth can feed the world- Jesus Christ. In the Old Testament, two animals could be the atonement of a nation. The realizing of one's potential in Christ could and will cause the world's, the nation's, the church's, and the neighborhood's viewpoints about Christianity to be changed forever just as with apostles Paul and Ruth.

Walking in the anointing of God, is believing, that God is always in control. Many a man or woman has sung "Oh how I love Jesus," and "Amazing Grace" on Sunday mornings only to despair about financial crises or strained family relationships on Sunday night. God can meet and answer any problems we have. Though we are human and have a disposition to worry and complain does not dispel the fact that we are sons and daughters of God, and our prayers can and will change things. When saints and churches begin to preach and believe in God's delivering power, then we will see the full glory of being servants of God. These days, God's sons and daughters have an expectation of God that is limited and pathetic. Everybody is on television or social media preaching the problem, but few are giving the solution. When you get into the face of God and He shows you a problem, do not be afraid to stay there. Get his solution, outlook, love, and boldness to be a problem solver for today's church and nation.

In Mark 10:15 the Bible says, *"Whosoever shall not receive the kingdom of God as a little child, he shall not enter therein."* Do you remember the passion with which you grasped and thought about circumstances and actions as a child? Nothing was too big to do or too simple to ask. You asked for and expected the world and were happy if the sun brightly shined or the snow lightly fell. Every sunny day was expected to yield new experiences and fun. Every winter day was supposed to be filed with 100 snowball fights and sledding. Have you forgotten? As a child the meteorologist's predictions or mother's thoughts that it might be too hot or cold for you to go outside did not amount to anything unless your freedom to go outside was taken from you.

You and I are saints upon salvation according to the Bible. (The word saint in Greek is hegios, meaning blameless, religious, or consecrated). We must realize who you are in Christ because we cannot walk proficiently in the anointing of God until we realize who we are. It is no wonder that men and women who have the power of God dwelling in them coward before Satan's people for fear of being accused of striving for perfection, but the Bible says otherwise in Hebrews 6:1 and 2 Corinthians 7:1. Saints striving for perfection is not optional for Christians. It is in fact a crucial part to being Christian. People have lowered their expectations of God because they have not been fed anointed words of God.

People get saved every day around the world because they heard the Word, accepted it, and confessed Jesus Christ as Lord and Savior. They initially go to church with a zeal to hear the message and praise God, but after a while they become resigned to trite sermons and music that lack the freshness of God and the blame can lie in the pulpit and choir stands. If people ministering do not spiritually know who they are, why should God move through them?

Not until ministers, choirs, and anyone else speaking God's Word realizes they are anointed enough to do all things in Christ, will the church make the difference God calls on us to make in people's lives today. We must stand up and be who the Bible says we are. Positionally in Christ we are blameless before God. Conditionally, daily, we are to walk in the Spirit to see this position actualized in daily living. Trying is a word for those who depend upon self. Doing and realizing, even without results, is what saints do. When saints do not live as saints, they confess their sin to God, accept the recompense from God, and keep living.

Many wonder why some Christians come out of anonymity to shine bright their light for Christ. The reason is because these Christians choose to believe they can make a difference in this world by being who God has called them to be. Churches have been around for centuries, but how many ministers or choirs expect to change lives every time they open their mouths because they know God's words that they are speaking will bring change? Not enough. Throughout the Bible, it has been the minority and not the majority that walks in the full anointing of God.

Self, unbelief, and sin limit us, yet all these things can be addressed with prayer, fasting, and obedience to God. Every Christian must expect more from God than themselves. People have become presidents, billionaires, inmates, and icons by depending on self. Realize your potential, calling, and appointment by and for God. Begin to stand up for God in your workplace, church, and wherever you may be. When you can say and believe that greater is He in you than any opposition, you can begin walking comfortably in the anointing of God.

Satan fears faith and works of God's people in Jesus Christ's name and power. To truly walk comfortably in the anointing of God, we must take up our spiritual weapons of armor: the sword, which is God's Word, the helmet of salvation, the breastplate of righteousness, the belt of truth, the sandals of peace, and send Satan fleeing from our homes, churches, and nation.

In Luke 50, scripture shares about a man's daughter who was pronounced dead, but when Jesus heard, he told the man not to fear but believe his daughter would be made whole. Jesus then proceeded to go to the man's house and awaken the daughter from death with the words, "Maid arise."

Arise saints! Arise ministers! Arise and know that you are the vessels of life, hope salvation, and love that God has chosen currently. Stop accepting less and wanting more. Begin by asking more of God, giving more to God, and believing you are a part of the more that is coming. Do not become frustrated by inadequacies of your character. You were created divinely and purposed elected. Your weaknesses are opportunities for demonstrations of God's strength. Your strengths are rooted God's grace. True saints are never satisfied with just salvation. It is the anointing that teaches, preaches, breaks yokes, and changes lives.

We are just vessels it comes through. You have got it, so use it! With God you can do all things. When you believe and walk in this truth in your life, you will see the power of God at work.

In life all things were created in and through God for a purpose; either you'll be a stone stepped on by the anointed, or an anointed stepper on the stones

reaching the stairway of heaven.

CHAPTER 8
So Close Yet So Far

"But, beloved, be not ignorant of this one thing, that one day is with the Lord as a thousand years, and a thousand years as one day. The Lord is not slack concerning his promise, as some men count slackness; but is long-suffering to us-ward, not willing that any should perish, but that all should come to repentance.

But the day of the Lord will come as a thief in the night; in which the heavens shall pass away with a great noise, and the elements shall melt with fervent heat, the earth also and the works that are therein shall be burned up." (2 Peter 3:8-10)

Oftentimes during life, we can become discontent with the way life seems to drag on. God sees the daily trials and problems that surround you. Day after day we question the value of life and how serving God rewarding. In this epistle of Peter, the writer attempts to stir up the pure minds of the saints. In this day, our minds need to also be stirred. Every day we get older and the monotony of lies becomes expected and boring. This is the kind of attitude that may be fine for those belonging to the world, but for Christians it is pathetic and not in line with God's will. We have daily got to have an expectation of hope in and from God.

Satan often distracts our minds from the reality of what God has for us and it can manifest in several different ways. For example, if we miss fifteen minutes of the preacher's sermon to help someone find a scripture, we are missing the words God gave the preacher specifically for us to hear. If we go to church to worship and praise God, but end up focusing on fashion, hairstyles, and other irrelevant thoughts, our focus is not where it needs to be to hear what God wants to say to us.

The world today is full of people sold out for Christ believing they are going to heaven, and yet daily deny God's power when they think God cannot work a certain way or allow a certain event to come to pass. It is a blessing that God does not act or think along our patterns of thoughts. We would all be dead and unredeemed. I praise God for his grace and mercy. God's mercy is so wonderful that to question God's validity as king of mercy is utter hypocrisy. The people of Jeremiah's day shared these common doubts about God when they said, *"The fathers have eaten a sour grape set end the children's teeth are set on edge,"* (Jeremiah 31:29).

The people then and now of the church focused on the fact that their personal sins did not seem to fit their present punishment or circumstance. Many are of the attitude that if so and so was living a sinful life behind the scenes and was exposed, then all the church problems were their fault. This is a lie from Satan. Just because a greater penalty in one's personal or church life falls when a certain sin unfolds, do not blame them. God just chose to begin to exercise the judgment at the discovery of this more public sin. We must stop judging and realize as Romans 5:20 says, *"Where sin abounded, grace did much more abound."*

Stop blaming and assuming. Start praying and fasting more. We can see the glory and reality of God's grace beyond Him giving us salvation if we will let Him use us as examples of how to walk in the power of His grace before one another.

Next time things get a little difficult, do not look around. Just find somewhere to bend your knees and/or heart to the Lord in prayer. From there it is all about God's leading you and not you are limiting Him (see Proverbs 3:5-6).

We are all sinners saved by grace, but there are thousands of churches that serve God by the letter of the law and not the spirit of the law when it comes to being accepting of others. Man, a church seems so close to God in holiness and worship. But, let the wrong race or a crudely dressed man or a woman wearing skin tight outfit enter, and we see truly how far the church is from God's commandment in James: *"For if there come unto your assembly a man with a gold ring,*

in goodly apparel, and there come in also a poor man

in vile raiment; and ye have respect to him that weareth

the gay clothing, and say unto him, Sit thou in a good

place, and say to the poor stand thou there, or sit here

under my footstool: Are ye not partial in yourselves, and

become judges of evil thoughts," (James 2:2-4).

Favoritism must be put to death along with partiality in our churches. A true servant of God will serve the monetary rich the same as the monetary poor or they are guilty of sin. Somehow Satan has placed prejudice on the rich too. People have fought so hard for economic equality and opportunity that they have forgotten that God is the key to blessings in all aspects of life. Men and women in the church will donate countless hours and funds to the poor of Mexico and Africa, but not many would visit the high schools of

Beverly Hills to share their time and the gospel of Jesus Christ. Christian's opinions of prejudice and equality are taking the form of the worlds.

True liberty is found in the Holy Spirit. Just because we are close to America's heart does not mean we are close to God's heart. While many programs and ministries dedicated to poverty-stricken countries are indeed needed, evangelism should not stop at the doors of aristocracy or the rich. If we will witness and pray for more of corporate America instead of just soliciting them, we would be closer to destroying Satan's kingdom and further from building it up through our ignorance.

The day of the Lord has been preached for centuries and because of this, people's hearts have become hardened thinking nothing matters if their good outweighs their bad. We cannot begin to comprehend God's grace, love, and mercy, but we also must remember that God is righteous. God's righteousness requires that there be punishment for sin and blessings for good. Unbelief on our part does not change the character or decisiveness of God's decisions.

We in the church must wakeup to the factors of sin being judged, eternity, and purpose. If God's judgment was seriously heeded, this nation would be full of churches zealous for the salvation of others and obedience to Christ inside their walls. Eternity cannot be numbered and as such we as ministers of God's Word have an advantage over any fears of the finite world.

God promises eternal life in peace. Satan and the world offer an eternity of fire. The choice for any sane individual is God. So why then is our nation seemingly choosing Satan? Purpose! The church is not giving people purpose. The Holy Spirit guides us, but often through others. Whether teaching the Word or preaching, the saints of God must give their actions purpose.

Pastors need to seek God's face more for sermons for youth and the church must be determined to be the foundation built upon the cornerstone of Jesus Christ in the lives of these youth.

"And, behold, one came and said unto him, Good Master, what good things shall I do, that I may have eternal life? And He (Jesus) said unto him, Why callest thou me good? There is none good but one, that is, God: but if thou wilt enter life, keep the commandments. The young man saith unto him, all these things have I kept from my youth up: what lack I yet? Jesus said unto him, If thou wilt be perfect, go and sell that thou hast, and give to the poor and thou shalt have treasure in heaven: and come and follow me."
(Matthew 19:16-17, 20-21)

The young man in this parable went away sorrowful because he did not choose the things of God over the things of Satan. Part of the wording of this parable in Mark says that Jesus beheld him and loved him. How many of us have been so close to God's riches and grace and yet so far because of self and the cares of the world? Though this young man is loved by Jesus and offered perfection, he chose the riches of the world.

My brothers and sisters of this present age, we must move beyond the act of confession unto salvation and perfection and on to expectation. We are children of God and therefore we have access to change lives and circumstances through prayer and deed. The Bible says that if our righteousness does not exceed that of the scribes and Pharisees, we shall in no case enter into the kingdom of heaven. In other words, it matters not how many people we have witnessed to, helped, or preached to. It is not enough. Our efforts outside of God can be used for good but we must do things God's way and in God's time to see God's results.

Let us begin to flex these muscles of God by submitting to and obeying the Holy Spirit. Nations were wiped out, lands conquered, and souls won by men and women of God who believed and walked in the power (not just the speech) of the kingdom of God. Dry messages and songs must give way to radical witnessing and Holy Spirit led services. For centuries Satan has used the tactic of intimidating Christians to conform to popularity to keep us from fully achieving our blood bought victory over him. Many churches have seen the compromising their institution and ministries through apostates or love of money. Hardly anyone will sound the alarm because of intimidation of Satan. Satan has disguises such as salaries, friends and various comfort zones such as job security and family approval.

"For there must be also heresies among you, that they which are approved may be made manifest among you." (1 Corinthians 11:19)

"Son of man, speak to the children of thy people, and say unto them, When I bring a sword upon a land, if the people of the land take a man of their coasts and set him for their watchman: but if the watchman see the sword come, and blow not the trumpet, and the people be not warned if the sword come, and take any person from among them, he is taken way in his iniquity; but his blood will I require at the watchman's hand." (Ezekiel 33:2,6)

Only the blood of Jesus can wash away our sin. Wash your hands, saints. Confess your sins. Repent from luke-warmness.

The Bible also says that many will die for a good man but none for a righteous one. John the Baptist and Jesus were hated because they spoke God's true Word and it convicted those who heard it. Woe to the Christian that is welcomed in every group and liked by all. Jesus was not. We as servants cannot be greater than the master. A friend of the world is an enemy of God's. Everyone wants to be liked or appreciated, but the favor that matters first is God's.

Sound the alarm. God has works for his people to do. It matters not if people tell you to take care of it later. Act now. Lives are in the balance, and you are accountable to God for them. Get into your prayer closet and seek God's face for boldness and opportunity to sound the alarm. Quit hoping someone else will do it or that God will work a miracle. You are the miracle and answer God has provided! You are the vessel for the salvation of others. God will use your fasts, your prayers, and your testimony. Do not doubt that God wants to use you!

Right now, I charge you in the name of Jesus Christ to be a part of change through witnessing, loving, and praying more. Sister Rahab in Joshua 2:1-16 and Hebrews 11:31 was not interested in looking holy before she put her life on the line for a God she had only heard about. If anybody might have found reason for self-condemnation, it was Rahab. She was a harlot who endangered her family by lying to the king. She spoke truth concerning God and boldly requested the lives of her family and their stuff be delivered from destruction and death. She, being who she was, seemed so close to death yet she was spared and then blessed to be a relative of Jesus Christ (see Matthew 1:5).

God wants to use you, but Satan wants to kill you. If the fact that a spiritual being is out to kill you, your family, and even children does not cause you to pick up your cross and fight the good fight, then what will? Many are close to God yet so far from walking in the power of God. What you lack, God is willing to give if you use those gifts for His purposes and by his leading.

"And the lord commended the unjust steward, because he had done wisely: for the children of this world are in their generation wiser than the children of the light." (Luke 16:8)

Jesus told this parable to illustrate a fact that the people of this world (Satan's children) often outsmart the children of light (God's children) in use of resources. Capone, by violence and manipulation, created an era of gang wars. Hitler, by speech and propaganda, almost took over the world.

What are you and I doing with the gospel of Jesus Christ? Language, politics, poverty, race, and denominations are not barriers that evil stops at. So, why is illiteracy and unbelief stopping the church from doing good? People will say that a man who cannot read anything, but the Bible is too illiterate to preach at their church, but composers and inventors who could not read the Bible have been given worldly acclaim and access to kings. Children are taught manners and/or cursing at an early age, but fasting and worshipping God waits until their older. Let us not any longer allow anything to impede us from righteousness. We must begin to use our jobs, experiences, intellect, and intangibles to bring people into God's kingdom.

If you cannot by prayer and faith find a way to be used by God, you should examine if you are in a relationship with God. The God I serve struck men dead and caused women to become diseased that thought regards to doing things for God without consulting God (See Numbers 12:1-16 & 16:1-50). Consulting God is as easy as asking Him to help you do his will. Mind you, there are times when it seems a bit harder than this but until you show yourself faithful in the small matters, how can He entrust larger matters to you?

"Take the rod, and gather thou the assembly together, thou and Aaron they brother, and. speak ye unto the rock before their eyes; and it shall give forth his water, and thou shalt bring forth to them water out of the rock: so, thou shalt give the congregation and their beasts to drink. And Moses took the rod from

before the Lord, as he commanded him. And Moses and Aaron gathered the congregation together before the rock and he said until them, Hear now, ye rebels; must we fetch you water out of this rock? And Moses lifted up his hand and with his rod he smote the rock twice: and the water came out abundantly, and the congregation drank, and their beasts also. And the Lord spoke unto Moses and Aaron: "Because ye believed me not, to sanctify me in the eyes of the children of Israel, therefore ye shall not bring this congregation into the land which I have given them."
(Numbers 20:8-12)

Has there ever been a man or woman who worked so hard and was so close to the promise land of God, yet so far away from fulfilling his dream of seeing it? I think not. Some people feel they have done enough for God so that He owes them something.

Granted, all do not consciously think this way, but even the majority who do not think it often act out this idea. We must constantly remember Proverbs 16:25 that says, *"there is a way that seemeth right unto a man: but the end thereof are the ways of death."*

When God gives us instructions, we must follow them to God's specifications. God says love thy neighbor as thyself. Are you? If you are not, then what do you expect God to do about this sin? We often wonder why God's Word doesn't seem to work in us, but it is working just like it says it will. The most important thing about an individual is if they are saved or not for nothing else has eternity hanging in the balance. Oh, that we as God's children would realize God wants obedience! Once Moses had disobeyed and God passed judgment, Moses did not plead or make excuses but lived with his mistake.

Christians often think God is too merciful to do certain things. Read your Bible. It matters not what public opinion says about God's judgments, but what the Bible says. No one can comprehend the mind of God. We have His Word, and this is the scope of our concrete understanding.

Why did Moses strike the rock instead of just speaking to it? Why do so many people seek to go around or over or ignore God's commands? The answer is a lack of faith in the totality of God's power.

Daily, Christians feel they can raise their kids by the world's standards and morals and have a sold-out child for Christ. This is not so. If you plant apple seeds, expect apples to grow. If you put the world's ways into your children, expect their desire for the world to grow. How many of your children or friends' children fast regularly? Excuses can be made but the bottom line is that God can sustain and nurture His people, especially children.

The church must place more stock in obedience than attendance. Accountability begins with the leadership of families and churches. Just as Moses allowed his frustration with the people to become a stumbling block to him, your own rash words and quick decisions could cause you not to enter the promised land. Do not take lightly the fact that God allowed you to lead His people as found in Luke 12:48b, *"For unto whomsoever much is given, of him shall be much required: and to whom men have committed much, of him they will ask the more."*

Men, women, children, family, and friends will ask and expect more of leadership. It is nothing new for more to be expected of leaders than others, but church leaders must realize that their accountability is possible earthly condemnation for failure. Mistakes are made daily by all of us. The results and punishments as God see fit. Chastisement is always unique to our God given revelations and abilities. God created us not in expectation of what we *might* do, but with a purpose of what we are *able* to and *should* do.

Instead of pastoring, some pastors might profit more by attending church and being the best witnesses they can be.. Just because you can speak well does not mean you are a pastor. Conversely, some people are sitting comfortably in church listening when they should instead be pastoring. Just because you feel inadequate leading people does not mean God has not called you to lead.

On judgment day, before God, you'll be held accountable for what He created you to do! Church leaders can live in denial of the facts of the Bible. It clearly states that disobedience and disrespect of persons will bring God's wrath down, yet these things run amuck in churches. Instead of church leaders identifying the problems, seeking God's face for the answer to the problem, and enacting the solution as God leads, they act as if they are blind to the facts.

Church is not for personal agendas and programs. It is to show God's wisdom (see Ephesians 2:10). The church does this by looking and acting like Christ, not the world we live in (see Romans 12:2). Life is just not about living out the dreams and expectations of self or others. It is about God's work.

Salvation should not only be stressed, but be the expectation of every book, song, and sermon. Once you are saved, ask God to use you to carry the message and purpose to others. Yes, there are needs of healing and learning for all Christians. Do the work of God and watch as work is done in you.

"For our light affliction, which is but for a moment, worketh for us a far more exceeding and eternal weight of glory. For we know that, if our earthly house of this tabernacle were dissolved, we have a building of God, a house not made with hands, eternal in the heavens. For in this we groan, earnestly desiring to be clothed upon with our house which is from heaven: For we know that the whole creation groaneth and travaileth in pain together until now." (2 Corinthians 4:17, 5:1-2, Romans 8:22)

Christians must realize, every fiber of goodness and desire to be heaven-complete in them is from God. When we get to heaven, we will receive resurrected bodies Christ did. God knows that our goal is heaven, but He also knows as humans we must actually feel and see ourselves accomplishing things for God. Those times when we feel, act, and look great, are the moments God is allowing us the rest and peace that comes with living in God's will. The trying and difficult moments of our walk with God are for our growth. These times also yield a plethora of new goals, steps for more obedient behavior, and a reality check that Earth is only our temporary home.

Men and women of great faith throughout the Bible were persuaded and confessed that they were strangers and pilgrims on the Earth! As you do the same, you declare plainly that you seek a country called heaven. You must realize and live knowing God as your Father said that Jesus Christ as your Savior gives you permission to enter a city prepared for you: a city of gold not in need of sun nor moon for the glory of God lighteth it. Your imagination cannot comprehend the beauty of Heaven God has for you, for it would pale in comparison. Satan has slowly but methodically dulled our expectations of Heaven and God. If this were not so, people would fear what God thought before what momma, daddy, boyfriend, or girlfriend thought. Ministers would not determine the length and content of messages by congregation's whims and attitudes, but by God's direction of the Holy Spirit. However, God has given us examples of how to truly defeat Satan:

- The Bible. The examples and Word of God are clear. In 1 Corinthians 10:11 the Bible says, *"Now all these things happened unto them for examples: and they are written for our admonition, upon who the ends of the world are come."* Having read this, how can you from this moment on deny that God has equipped you with the power of the Holy Spirit and battle strategies found in scripture to walk victoriously over Satan?

- Let God lead you. A key to Israel's victories over their adversaries was allowing God to fight for them. God can use any means including human, animal, and even Heavenly Host to accomplish victory. The key is inviting God into the fight and asking Him to lead you in whatever manner He sees fit. How often God would like to spare His people (Yes!) from misery and frustration, but because of our lack of giving the problem over to Him He allows us to falter until we surrender to His Will? *"But their minds were blinded: for until this day remaineth the same vail untaken away in the reading of the Old Testament, which vail is done away in Christ,"* (2 Corinthians 3:14).

- Witness. I believe every Christian that has done any kind of witnessing has run into an individual who plainly could not understand the simplicity of the gospel. Many Christians blame themselves for not being able to quote scripture better or speak better to be a witness for Jesus

Christ. I tell you that if all you know is that God is love and God tells you to witness, God will use and work through you. It is God who does all the work.

Jesus told some of the Jewish people who were upset with Him that they could not understand his speech for they could not hear his Word. There was a veil over their understanding as there still is a veil over most of the world's understanding of God. The only way this will change is when people hear, believe, accept, and confess the gospel of Jesus Christ in faith.

Why should God reveal Himself to anyone who won't by faith accept Him as Lord of their lives? We will never know the wonder, conviction, love, and peace of God until you surrender to Him. Choose this day not to settle for a form or idea of who you think God is. To understand God, you must accept God. Close counts for nothing when eternity is your destination! Accept

Jesus Christ as your Lord and Savior today to rededicate your life to Jesus Christ and ask for a renewed mind and spirit.

Chapter 9
What Name Are You Called By

"That at the name of Jesus every knee should bow, of things in Heaven and things in Earth, things under the Earth." (Philippians 2:10)

A name, a name, what is in a name? Many a man or woman has come into this world given a name that suits the tastes or beliefs of his or her parents. But when God called us His sons and daughters, He made a decree and announcement to hell. These are the vessels through which I will tear down your kingdom and schemes. These are chosen children of mine, to whom I have given authority and wisdom and have predestined to defeat you. Come out, come out wherever you are, children of the King. Come out of your bouts of failure and/or addiction. Come out from the world of conformity to a life of peculiarity. Be not what you feel or think, but what God called you to be.

Throughout life, we are known by many names - infant, good kid, active kid, bright teenager, troubled teenager, young adult, businessman, laborer, sinner, troublemaker, mentor, grandparent, etc. We often identify with these labels over the identity of who God calls us to be. Children of light, sheep, and saints are the identities God has given us.

Oh, that each of us would look beyond mere syllables and pronunciation of words to realize the divine choice God made when He named us. Do you not know that God knew you before the foundation of the world? Please realize that you could not have been disposed of or been a mistake. Your name was known before your first thought. It is no wonder that from each baby's inception into the world Satan has manipulated society into naming the child before dedicating it to Christ.

Take notice of how many "How or What to Name your Baby" books are on the market today. You have religious people wanting you to name the child from the Bible. You have races of people saying that is a black name or a white name. The intellectual community is telling you what the surveys say are the most effective names for future success. Today, the world gives glory to many names when only the name of Jesus Christ casts out demons, changes lives, and can (by acceptance or rejection) condemn or justify an individual before God.

"And there were seven sons of one Sceva; a Jew and chief of the priests, which did so. And the evil spirit answered and said, Jesus I know, and Paul I know; but who are ye." (Acts 19:14-15)

Who are you? Satan asks you this every day. "Who are you?" the evil spirit asks you through commercials that entice you to lust. "You are a failure and a disappointment," Satan whispers when people degrade you. This scripture in Acts 19 goes on to say that the man in whom the evil spirit lived leaped on them, overcame them, and prevailed against them so that they fled out of that house naked and wounded.

You can claim to be a Christian and do all the right things people think a Christian should do, but when the devil or his demons put their focus on you it is only the power of Jesus Christ in you that will protect you. It is only the name of Jesus Christ that strikes fear and brings victory over Satan.

Many an individual believes that self-will or even tragedy has brought them victory over addictions such as drinking or smoking. Just because you survived difficulties does not mean you have victory in this area of your life. Surviving in and of itself is not what makes us victors.

I want you to realize: these men tried to use Jesus' name but did not really know him as their Lord and Savior, so they were overcome by the evil spirit. Without a true relationship with Jesus as your Lord and Savior, you will not tear down the strongholds in your life or overcome the manifestations of evil spirits.

Satan outwits smokers by changing the addiction from a bag of weed to compulsive gambling. Satan changes the addiction of alcohol to one of pride. Though the spirits of Satan's army, change may come but will end in a new addiction or challenge whose objective is your defeat and death.

Very few people are overcome physically by demon-possessed people, but how many families and lives have been left naked, wounded, and overcome by poverty, lust, greed, and lack of God? What political party, gang, or social class has met Satan on the battlefield and won?

We strive to be associated with and called so many titles such as minister or president that can be good names to have but do not necessarily equal victory over Satan. I have seen men defeated by turmoil and women's self-worth destroyed because they put faith in titles.

The key to finding your name as a child of God is surrendering our lives to Jesus Christ AND believing he is sovereign enough to fight our battles and win against Satan. In chapter 20 of 2 Chronicles, a King named Jehoshaphat faces overwhelming odds. He could call on the Egyptians or mercenaries or false gods to save him and Judah as his predecessors did, but he did not. He called upon God and the result was victory. They won the battle by singing praises to the Lord. As they praised God, the enemy began to strike and eventually destroy one another.

Now that is a miracle.

The God of the Old Testament is the same God of the New Testament. Though He manifested Himself into the earthly form of Jesus Christ, He was the same God. You must give God your battles against Satan.

Have you ever tried to fight the wind with your thoughts? Have you ever tried shaking your head in church to push last night's indiscretions out of your mind? This never works and ultimately only leaves people feeling defeated and exasperated from attempting to fight Satan without Jesus Christ in them as Lord and Savior.

Some have made Jesus their Savior, but not their Lord. When you say, "Jesus is my Lord," you are saying you will daily conform to His Godly image, will allow Him to fight your battles, and will be obedient to his Word even when it seems as if it is not working. Realize that the major difference between faith in God and belief in God is that faith is from God whom even demons even believe in but do not have faith in (see 2 Thess. 3:2 & Jan. 2:19). Faith is living and believing God's Word even when conditions and circumstances say otherwise (see Hebrews 11:1). When you say Jesus is your Savior and Lord you are saying you cannot do anything alone and will not win any victory that is without Christ in you. In Christ, all the victories can be yours because he will gladly fight your battles.

People will say Jesus saved them from this world but then turn around and say God cannot help them with this problem. Messages from our pulpits do not typically say God is not capable of answering every need, but through actions and words they imply that God has restrictions and limitations in our lives.

It is no wonder that young people today rebel against church. If we as parents do not place everything in God's hands, why should they? Honor the Lord Jesus Christ not just in name but in allowing him through word and action to have dominion over and in your life.

Throughout the history of the Bible, numerous people have looked to man rather than God. Conventional principles and thoughts have cost people miracles and added undue complication to the instructions of God. When Moses struck the rock instead of speaking to it, he demonstrated a lack of faith. Believing God in name alone is not enough. You must believe the power of that name and act in accordance. In 2 Kings 5:1-4 Naaman was given simple instructions on how to be cured from his leprosy, but because the instructions were so simple Naaman doubted and complained about them before he ever obeyed.

"And his servants came near, and spake unto him, and said, My father, if the prophet had bid thee do some great thing, wouldest thou not have done it? How much rather then when he saith to thee, Wash, and be clean?" (2 Kings 5:13)

Because Naaman was told something as simple as go and wash in Jordan seven times to be cured of this terrible disease, he not only doubted but also became dissatisfied with the cure God chose to use. We people of this time find so many ways to try to be cured of things. The Bible states throughout that God (Jesus Christ) is the answer. Picture going home or to church and telling the people there that if they would all cry out to God with a pure heart, their problems would be tended to as never before. You would see frowning, doubting, and blank facial expressions. You might see a glimmer in others' countenance. What would be yours?

Being a Christian is not just falling under a religious heading. It is living day after day bearing your cross, shining a bright light, and being conformed to the image of God. Bearing your cross is carrying others' hopes and burdens to Jesus because they have not or cannot. Shining as a bright light is being all the Bible tells you to be righteous, holy, loving, etc. Being conformed to the image of God always means asking God to mold you into what He created you to be as well as listening and obeying the thoughts, commands, and leading of the Holy Spirit.

"And when they had set them in the midst, the asked, by what power, or by what name, have ye done this?" (Acts 4:7)

Have you ever been in the midst and then asked by what power or what name have ye done this? In other words, have you ever been surrounded by something or someone people would question being in the presence of a Christian? To be brought into a midst as a Christian means whomever the bystanders are, they have an expectation of you.

The people of God expect to be captivated, given direction, and told of the things they can obtain by obeying God. It is not so much that all are greedy for blessings but that they need an expectation of fulfillment in obeying God's will.

The people of Satan expect a show of the weaknesses and failures of Christians' faith and obedience. For when Satan's people can bathe in the deception that a child of God has failed, they will. This is because without the seeming failure of a Christian, there is no victory or substance to their sad lives. Without the constant mirage that Christians often fail, how would Satan keep you from God's provision and promises for you once you accepted Him into your life?

All of us are fearfully and wonderfully made (see Psalm 139:14). Our names do not just represent a few letters of the alphabet in random order. They represent a glimpse of the potent powers of God. Ask me your purpose, but first assume the name of saint (separated) rather than sinner (someone who misses the mark set by God, a rebel against God, a perverter of something from its natural use).

A saint, from Philippians 4:21, is someone who is sacred, physically pure; morally blameless, ceremonially consecrated, and most holy. A sinner, as defined by John 9:31, is someone who misses the mark (so not share in the prize). These definitions are from the Greek meanings of saint and sinner in the context given. Thus, the person with the sinful attitude has separated themselves from God, while those with righteous attitudes and trust in Christ have united with God.

We all sin but if you have accepted Christ, it is your free choice and no longer your natural affinity. After you accept Jesus Christ as your Lord and Savior, choose to live for God. Humble yourself under God's mighty hand and claim the name of son or daughter or servant of God and stand in contrast to the names of worldly conquerors. Adjectives such as promising, prominent, and professional are often associated with those who the world deems acceptable. Adjectives such as fervent, zealous, patient, and holy are terms used by God to describe His people's character. The first set will do here on earth, but pale in comparison to those given in heaven. What adjectives describe you?

Know that the name and description you are abiding under right now has eternal ramifications. Do not take lightly the labels or names that represent your character.

All my life, I lived by a set of names that seemed to bring about pain, pressure, depression, and aggression. Satan kept me blind to the man God called me to be. I sold out so cheaply for the things of this world that to mention my price would give Satan far too much credit and glory. Since accepting Jesus Christ into my life, I've been becoming the man God predestined me to be.

Psalm 76:10 is the true essence and reality of this world. God will get the praise no matter what. Even if it is drawing your family to hear the Word of God at your funeral despite the fact you did not live for God.

When speaking of the wrath of God and the correlation of it with the name you wear (God's child or Satan's), I speak of wrath that causes godly sorrow and brings eternal damnation. If you have salvation, you have at some point in your life experienced godly sorrow. This is a sorrow that causes a person to not only want a change to be better and establish a relationship with God, but also gives you the desire to do your part to bring this about. If you currently have no relationship with God, you are no doubt experiencing an inner emptiness that can only be compared to the emptiness of a black hole in space. A black hole exists but for what purpose for those of us who live miles away from it?

Daily, people walk, talk, and function in this world without being touched by others. I am not speaking about the kind of touch that is physically felt through casual contact or sensual passions. I am speaking of the touch of the heart.

If your perspective is gloomy and your heart's thoughts feel like a prison of denial, God is the only remedy. When was the last time you cried out and prayed to God? The violence, callousness and deceptions of this world have created a spiritual war zone in us. Please note, there can be no compromises or truces with Satan. The time has come to accept the grace of God that is freely given. Grace is not obtained through works but is given freely. The only thing you must do is accept this grace from God. Are you tired of all the names this world has categorized you with? Step out in faith. Call on the name of the Lord Jesus and ask God to help you accept His grace. Surrender to His Will and let God establish a good name for you before Him in this world.

"Either make the tree good, and his fruit good; or else make the tree corrupt, and his fruit corrupt: for the tree is known by his fruit." (Matthew 12:33)

"And the child Samuel ministered unto the Lord before Eli and the word of the Lord was precious in those days, there was no open vision." (1 Samuel 3:1)

God is not a respecter of persons. This truth alone has saved some people and condemned others. Those whom God chooses to respond to His revelations were chosen for no other reason than God's grace and mercy. Those who were not chosen by God to be a part of the kingdom of heaven cannot by good deeds, money, or influence enter the gates of Heaven.

We as God's creation need to realize that it is God and God only who gives good things and is in control of all things. In a time when hearers and speakers of God's Word were few and highly esteemed; God called a boy named Samuel. God called Samuel three times in an audible voice (see 1 Samuel 3:1-10).

This story personifies many people's experiences with God. A schoolteacher, Sunday school teacher, coach, grandmother, or mother may have told us God has a plan and purpose for us. So many times, through miraculous saving grace, God has called us through difficult circumstances like the near fatal car accident, the life-threatening disease or infirmity, the suicidal depression, a broken heart, etc. These were calls God initiateed toward to us.

Just like Samuel, we can sometimes run to someone or something else thinking they or it was the originator of the call. We may answer to drugs, fornication, or false religions. The ironic part is that the priest in the story, Eli, was having all kinds of problems but still was a rope bearer to Samuel becoming closer to God.

The prostitute, the fallen minister, the wayward wife, the drug addict, or the alcoholic can still be instruments in getting you into an intimate relationship with God. Never allow your carnal perceptions of God's creation (people) to blind you from allowing God to use his creation (people) in your life. I praise God that many of us have answered God's call without having to be put through something to realize it was a loving God who was calling them. Many are called, but few are chosen.

Believe the Word of God is true. Accept the gospel of Jesus having come to die for your sins, was killed by crucifixion on the cross, was buried, arose on the third day, and ascended into Heaven, and sitteth on the right hand of God the Father in Heaven.

In Jesus' name I pray the end of any demonic forces from stealing God's words in this book from you, the reader. In Jesus' name, I command demons of doubt, disbelief, and the Anti-Christ to loosen. In Jesus' name, I lose hope, faith, belief, reassurance, and the convicting power of the Holy Spirit upon each reader.

Pray aloud: Lord, in Jesus' name, I pray and ask you to help me overcome all that has or would hinder me from answering the call you have placed on my life. I need and want your help to be who you created me to be in Jesus' Name. Amen.

Do people around you know you to be a Christian? The Word of God says we are to be lights to this world. If there is an individual whom you are acquainted with that does not know you are a Christian, you need to rectify the situation this day. In our society, it is not popular to be known as a Christian because people begin to expect more from you. Names such as fanatic, perfectionist, and Holy Roller have become synonymous with sold out to God Christians. Do not allow Satan's barrage of insults and sarcasm to dissuade you from being a light to others.

Take a candle for instance. When you light a candle in a dark place, the darkness flees from the light. No matter if the candle is as small as five inches in length and one inch in diameter and the dark area is the length and width of a football field, the light will repel the darkness in proportion to its size. You now have a basic understanding of what your light in God can accomplish to combat this evil world.

The name you are called by will dictate a lot of how people think about you in this world, but for God, the name you are called by determines where you spend eternity. Heaven or Hell. Two places. Two different destinations. Which do you choose? Not in name alone, but in action and word?

Know that because you call on Jesus and call yourself a Christian, life does not cease to be a series of ups and downs. No, but with the Spirit of God indwelling and teaching you and I, all of the experiences in our lives work to mature us in Christ. God has a goal in mind for us. Believe and stand firm on this truth. God works in our lives for the best.

Many Christians find themselves offended at the scriptures and truths preached from the pulpit. Why? Could it be that once people accepted the salvation God gives they begin to think they do not need God 's leading and helping? Or could it be that Christians' expectations of themselves in Christ is so far below the calling God has placed upon their lives that nothing they do satisfies the Spirit within them because they carry the name of conqueror but walk in the defeat of the stolen identity Satan deceived them with?

Just because we make the decision to accept salvation and be a child of God does not mean we are above or below who the Word of God says we are. When people hear we as Christians are to be holy, sanctified, and righteous in all areas of their life's congregations, some begin to judge the preachers of the messages in greater severity than they do themselves. This is scriptural. James 3:1 says that many should not be masters, knowing that they shall receive the greater condemnation. The only problem is that the same congregation does not want to live up to 1 Peter 2:9 which says, *"But ye are a chosen generation a royal priesthood, an holy nation, a peculiar people; that ye should shew forth the praises of him who hath called you out of darkness into his marvelous light."*

Did I misquote the scripture? Did I add to or take away from the scripture? No.

So why does a nation with King James Bibles such as what I quoted, not believe, or obey this scripture? The Christian walking with these words in his or her heart has a light in them that keeps the churches alive and growing.

Jesus' name is the name every knee will bow, and every tongue confess to. Jesus' name describes before time before it existed as "I Am."

We anger at the inconsistencies and failures of one another, forgetting that God is our master, and everyone gives account to Him. For if God was like man in His forgiveness, who would be in Heaven? We throw names on one another like the sands of dunes moved by powerful current. When we say sentiments such as:

- "He let me down, that fake so and so."
- "She said this, but she is nothing but a liar."
- "You have not accomplished anything yet. You are lazy."
- "I expected you to say that you are a hypocrite."

Names are cars for spirits, and the church of Jesus Christ throughout time has given some demons Bentleys to ride in. Peter lied, Abraham was a walking dead man before God manifested His true importance to him, Sampson seemed to let a nation down, Rahab was a harlot before she got it right with God. These people were called mighty, a rock of the church, a woman of faith, and a father of nations.

The world, your family, and friends, call you by many names: brother, sister, husband, and provider, but the only name that is everlasting is the one God gives you when you become one of His children. Once God adopts you into His heavenly family, then the work He uses and allows you to do on earth will last. Take heed parents and siblings. All the advice, discipline, and manners instilled into a child or close relative, will not stop one demon from destroying someone close to you in life. The fight is spiritual and unless you are prepared and are covered in Christ, then you lose. Just look at how many well-mannered, disciplined individuals are on drugs or living in the streets or are incarcerated.

Adults of today tend to waiver between two extremes. One group can take too much responsibility for younger generations. Another group who lives in shackles of denial, bitterness, and false truths takes no responsibility for the example they set for the next generation. Both sides must realize their responsibility begins when they put their decisions, children, and relatives in God's hands. For until they do this, it is like the blind leading the blind. This can strike some nerves, but the truth is evident from the Bible. Throughout the scriptures, tragedy after tragedy occurred until people placed their lives in God's hands.

This may leave some of you wondering about children who were raised in Christian homes. The only answer God gave me is found in Proverbs 22:6, *"Train up a child in the way he should go: and when he is old, he will not depart from it."* The Christian having family problems must believe Romans 8:28 which says, *"And we know that all things work together for good to the that love God, to them who are the called according to his purpose."*

As a person ages, the realities of what is right and wrong shines as a searchlight from a lighthouse in the dead of night. I know from my own experiences age can change one's perspective on life. As an adolescent, I wanted to explore and understand friends and myself. As a teenager, I wanted the experience of seeking independence and sensuality. In my late twenties, I became more settled into the mold that my choices made me. From age thirty-one on up, I have had the perspective of living out the wisdom God instilled in me as a child. This said, age in terms of spiritual understanding is not readily shown in numerical fashion, but in terms of choices, surrendering to God, and embracing God's will for one's life.

Some lifetimes span a short time here on Earth but transfer into an eternity while leaving benefit for others behind. Never give up, for God's eyes search the Earth - the whole Earth - for people whose hearts are perfect toward Him.

"For the eyes of the LORD run to and for throughout the whole earth, to skew himself strong in the behalf of them whose heart is perfect toward him. Herein thou hest done foolishly: therefore, from henceforth thou shalt have war." (2 Chronicles 16:9)

Continue to pray not blame. Get into God's Word more. Find a scripture or several and stand on them for help with your children, loved ones, or anyone, and watch as God takes the few scriptures you bring to Him and transforms them into hundreds of blessings for others.

Elijah did it for the widow with God's help (read 1 Kings 17:8-16). Jesus did it for the multitudes that followed him (see John 6:2-14). If oil can be multiplied and bread multiplied, then the scriptures that we share with family and others can be multiplied too.

Believe God is awesome enough not just to save your son or daughter but use them to rescue the grandmother or uncles who you have not been able to reach. Have faith! Believe God is going to answer your prayers and more abundantly than for what you ask.

Thank Him now for doing more in your life than you could possibly ask. Maybe you asked for salvation, and He gave you that and a mansion in Heaven. Maybe you asked for deliverance from something and in response He gave you an addiction for Him.

If it was not for God's goodness and mercy, you would not be alive. When did you ask to be born? So do not be so presumptuous to think you will choose when you die! Live a life in submission to God, not doubting or second-guessing Him. The key to living lawfully before God in spirit and in truth is believing in and trusting that God is sovereign.

In every instance of your life, know that God is helping you. God only desires the best for you, but please note I did not say you would understand or like it all. We all can at times act like selfish, ignorant people but if we got everything we wanted, what condition would our lives be in?

Bearing the name child of God is a great responsibility. Daily we must be a witness to others, for our witness may be the only example of who God is all about to others.

Most have heard the children's story of the boy who cried wolf. The boy, who was a shepherd of sheep constantly became bored. In becoming bored, he decided to pretend a wolf was trying to steal the sheep. He would cry out, "Wolf!" when there was none, and the people would come running to rescue the boy. One day a real wolf came. When the boy cried for help, nobody came. The wolf carried away the sheep and the boy learned a valuable lesson.

Christians are like this boy. We daily say we are more than conquerors as children of God and warriors against Satan. Yet, often, we are complaining and living in fear of Satan. So, when hard times come to people outside the church, it is no great wonder that false religions teaching immoral values and sermons with no conviction by the Holy Spirit attract people. Christians must begin to live a victorious life over Satan. We must become a people known as dependable, honest, and zealous to please God.

What are people's opinions about you? Do people fear the words of your mouth because they resound of truth and conviction? Do you bear the sword of the living Word of God in holiness and righteousness? Or do you bear a dagger of backbiting, deceit, and babblings of foolishness?

Your witness is the wolf. Though it is spoken about throughout the world and causes a stir of anticipation and wonder, until you show up in the power and authority of Jesus Christ (God), your witness demeans and hampers others who would come to Christ. If you being a professed Christian walk, talk, and act the same as the unsaved of the world, why would anyone seek out the one (God) whom you serve? They won't. Worse yet, the lambs which are the unstable, unsaved, lost souls of this world will be carried away by Satan.

Uphold the name of Christian in righteousness and humility. Our failures are opportunities for us to allow our Father (God Almighty) to be alive, needed, and intimate with us. It is far easier to be called a Christian than to be one. Allow God to be glorified in you by continually surrendering your will to God's. Two points to remember about a Christian that are unchangeable: to be a Christian one must have believed in and accepted Jesus Christ as Lord and Savior, and one will bear more good things than bad to help others.

Chapter 10
Walking in the Fire and Flags

One of the most taught lessons from childhood is do not play with fire. There is something about the flames of fire that excite the curiosity of most children. No matter how many times a child is told not to play with fire, it is not until they are burned, or get close enough to the heat to become leery of its source that they realize the danger and/or feel the pain of disobedience.

Why out of many of the things God created and used does fire hold a distinguishable place in the Bible? Fire goes from being symbolically used as a refiner of people to describing consuming eternal judgment to a representation of the Holy Spirit to a tool of destruction used by God. Fire is spoken of in the Bible numerous times but its spiritual, physical, or symbolic meaning depends upon the context of scripture surrounding the word.

When you think you have seen fire used to do everything God wills, you also find out that fire can represent a set of circumstances where change and growth takes place in people's lives where in the physical and spiritual fear of God, faithful people are brought into an abundant harvest of blessings.

What I find particularly interesting is the hypnotic attraction fire holds on people and the fact that it burns the impurities out of things. Fire, at times, helps reveal value as it simultaneously refines.

Walking in the spiritual fires of life has never been and will never be easy. Some of us even wonder why people must walk through these fiery trials. God is so awesome that He can take an element such as fire and physically save us:

"And the LORD went before them by day in a pillar of a cloud, to lead them the way; and by night in a pillar, of fire, to give them light; to go by day and night: He took not away the pillar of the cloud by day, nor the pillar of fire by night, from before the people. And the angel of God, which went before the camp of Israel, removed and went behind them; and the pillar of the cloud went from before their face, and stood behind

them: And it came between the camp of the Egyptians and the camp of Israel; and it was a cloud and darkness to them, but it gave light by night to these: so that the one came not near the other all the night." (Exodus 13:21-22 and 14:19-20)

"And there appeared unto them cloven tongues like as of fire, and it sat upon each of them. And they were all filled with the Holy Ghost, and began to speak with other tongues, as the Spirit gave them utterance." (Acts 2:3-4)

Human nature is to succumb to peer pressure and not make waves against the status quo. By allowing mental, physical, and spiritual fiery trials to come, God helps us to mature to a level of faith in Him in the fire that under normal circumstances we would not.

(Genesis 19:24). In Genesis 19:24, the word fire is used in a context that conjures images of an angry God who demands obedience and punishes disobedience as it describes how He brought brimstone and fire from heaven. Do you find it odd that out of all the ways the word fire is used in the Bible one use of it mentioned early on is as a weapon of destruction? You may have a better understanding of why when you realize one of the last usages of the word fire is to describe the second death. The second death spoke about in Revelation 21:8 says that the fearful, unbelieving, abominable, murderers, whores mongers, sorcerers, idolaters, and liars will have their part in the lake which will burn with fire and brimstone.

Eternal Destruction

I do not know about you, but from my observations these prerequisites to getting into the lake of fire are met by many who live in this world. I once was included in that group but because of God's grace I no longer have a reservation there. I believe God wants us to have a godly fear and reverence of His commands and judgments.

Sometimes I hear people say that they cannot believe a loving God would cast them into a lake of fire. I think these people forget the fact that God is just and honorable. God is not like man when it comes to honoring certain circumstances and certain people. For God to be truly as loving as these same people believe, He must have a fitting punishment for evildoers. His love is not just a whim, romance, or conditional convenience. God loves us so much that He sent His

Son. Jesus Christ to die for the world so our sins could be forgiven if we placed our faith in His Son.

What father or mother who loves their child as themselves does not take seriously anything that hinders or harms this child? Show me one father who has a lovely daughter that if she were raped and murdered would not want the transgressor caught and brought to justice. Granted, you may have a vast number of different punishments wanted by the father. Look deeply into a few more details of this scenario. There exists at the time of this violent act a set of laws and one punishment for all who are found guilty of this transgression and do not repent. The judge is the creator of integrity, honesty, and wisdom. He has never been wrong about the guilt or innocence of an individual. The judge has even tried through people and programs throughout the world to reform and bring the transgressor or transgressors to repentance and a change of mind. Now, having all this information can you truly with a clear conscience tell me that the father of the girl would not be justified in approving the punishment of the transgressor knowing all these facts?

It is worth pointing out that anyone who not only sins themselves, but influences others to do so as well and does not repent, is going to the lake of fire (see Revelation 20:15). The Bible says what it says, it matters not if you believe it. The sky, space, and the Earth were not created by your beliefs or disbeliefs. God said it and so it was. God beckons throughout scripture to repent and accept salvation or spend eternity in the lake of fire. You must realize that the Bible is God's Word. You cannot place faith in the salvation part of the Bible and believe in Heaven and then not believe the judgment part of the Bible. In

Romans 3:4 it says, *"Let God be true, but every man a liar."*

The penalty God has set in place for sin is death or the separation of spirit and soul from the physical body and separation from worshipping and fellowshipping with God. Every man and woman's thinking has been poisoned by sin since Adam and Eve. Knowing then what God's Word says and how for a lifetime we must seek God to have proper thinking, we can rightly say that thinking not lined up with God is from the devil. God says live. The devil says die. God says………………………………………………………..obey. The devil says disobey. God says there is a lake of fire where people will be cast. You say you are not sure. A person can play, look, and speak the part of a Christian but if God says one thing and you say another, you speak and represent your father the devil (see John 8:43-47).

Realize that another lie of Satan's is that God did not say lake of fire, but man did. My personal response to this is that the same writers in the Bible who inform you about eternal fire also inform you about salvation. A good tree cannot bare bad fruit and a bad tree cannot bare good fruit. God hates sin. God hates sin because it is the opposite of who He is and can cause the death of His children. God manifested Himself into the form of Jesus Christ in the flesh to bring life. Satan manifests himself into every kind of wickedness, perversion, and abomination to bring death.

Consuming Example

God used a donkey to speak and a virgin to bring the Savior into the world, but two examples that in sight alone brought distinction and glory to God were engineered by fire.

"And the angel of the Lord appeared unto him in a flame of fire out of the midst of a bush: and he looked, and behold, the bush burned with fire, and the bush was not consumed." (Exodus 3:2)

Can you imagine coming home late from work one night, looking in your backyard and seeing a bush on fire but not consumed? What would be your reaction? Bring out the water hose? Grab the fire extinguisher?

This example may seem improbable to you, but realize Moses was in an environment like home is to you. He was in the mountainous desert where bushes sometimes caught on fire and burned due to the severe heat. This was an everyday occurrence in the desert.

How many homes are merely resting places? Just like Moses' backyard desert, our homes are places of unfulfilled potential and numerous responsibilities. Hopefully you see how this incident could happen to you or I in our everyday homes. Accidents happen every day that should have ended in tragedy but did not. We can easily identify the sensationalism of a burning object not consumed but the scripture takes it further to identify the grace of God when we did not go insane after living through what we did at home.

"And Moses said I will now turn aside, and see this great sight, why the bush is not burnt. And when the Lord saw that he turned aside to see, God called unto him out if the midst of the bush, and said, Moses, Moses. And he said, Here am I." (Exodus 2:3-4)

God used the non-consuming fire to grab Moses' attention. It was not just the fire that interested Moses. It was the fact a fire, something he was used to seeing destroy things, was having no effect on a bush that should have been consumed. Just as God captured Moses' attention in this way, He also captures our attention.

Have you ever been pressed from every side by worries like: family turmoil, drugs, fornication, or illness? I want you to know these fires were allowed not to destroy you, but to grasp your attention. God would not allow something to enter your life to destroy you. God has a purpose for everything He allows to take place in your life. I am speaking to those doing the will of God, the sick child, the person who lost their job, the individual with an addiction to pornography. We are all able to overcome because of God.

"Blessed be God, even the father of our Lord Jesus Christ, the father of mercies, and the God of all comfort who comforteth us in all our tribulation, that we may be able to comfort them which are in any trouble, by the comfort wherewith we ourselves are comforted of God." (2 Corinthians 1:3-4)

Just drop to your knees and say, "Here I am, Lord." God does not just allow Satan to run wild in and out of your life. You are that bush. Though the flames burn intensely and all around, do you wonder how you stand around people without lifetime scars?

The fire is the Lord. Though the fires of circumstances can seem overwhelming, know that God is there. He needed to grasp your attention and do it in such a way you knew it was Him. The dog dying, mama passing away around age 80, and an argument here or there was not enough. The callous circumstances hardened Moses and perhaps they have hardened you too. So, God must do the amazing by allowing the circumstance, yet God engineered them to take place.

Take a few minutes to read Daniel 3 and learn about Shadrach, Meshach, and Abednego being thrown into a fiery furnace but untouched by the fire. God could have easily allowed the three young men not to be thrown into the flames, but He chose to allow it. Scrutinize the scriptures story a little deeper. Upon further inspection, it becomes evident that the fire was not so much for the testing of the three men's faith, but for the kings. If God sent angels to deliver the men, the glory may not have been as great for God.

Imagine everyone looking at the flames glow as three mighty men's bodies are hurled into the burning fire. There had to be an excitement and expectation amongst the onlookers. The anger and hatred of the king was great until suddenly he arose and testified that he saw *four* men in the fire. The king's word was law. His witness was as iron before the people. He even said that the form of the fourth was like the Son of God.

God was with Shadrach, Meshach, and Abednego in the fire and has been with you in the fire too.

When the king ordered the men to come out, not one of them showed signs of having been in the fire at all. The king's court was surely buzzing with the news. How could these men have survived if the fire was that hot? How were these men not hurt?

If you find yourself surrounded by doubters who doubt God and say the flames will overtake you,

tell them your God *can* deliver you and even if He does not, you will never testify that there is another god like Him.

I have felt the flames of the fire many times in my own life. There were days I was consumed in the flames of loneliness, anger, insecurity, and confusion. I kept my eyes on the Lord. I remembered that with every temptation and increase of the heat, God's grace and strength insulated me. People witnessed at times my bewildered expressions, distant answers, and fierce tone of voice. They did not know it at the time, but truly they were like the Babylonian king. They were viewing me in the consuming spiritual fires of God. Those who had the Spirit of God knew and, by faith, saw Jesus' walking with me. How do I know? Because I did not receive a hug or loving word of comfort. Instead, I received more of God's work to do, harder problems to pray and deal with, and fierce attacks from God's enemies. If my brothers in Christ had not seen Jesus with me, then they certainly would have covered me through the fires with the strength of God in them.

Please take note that when you are in the fire and it seems like spiritually you are comforted yet physically being torn apart, God is not only there but He is doing a work that took fire to consume you and grab the attention of an unbelieving world.

C. A Refiner Not Easily Understood

"But who may abide the day of his coming? and who shall stand when he appeareth? for he is like a refiner's fire, and like fullers' soap." (Malachi 3:2)

Have you ever been through a difficult situation for no apparent reason? Some days I have awakened praising God and did not experience another peaceful moment until I laid down that night to go to sleep. I had problems with my mouth, my friends, people I don't know, and even the food I had eaten upset me. From the moment these things began to happen, I was rebuking Satan and asking God to forgive me for any sin I might be suffering for. The strange thing is, I did not get peace, but more problems. I knew this was not scriptural. I began examining my faith. I found it was not wavering.

Should I stop now because what I experienced none of you have? Well, I'll go on for those who the Spirit is speaking to. God was not silent through it all, but He was not giving me full understanding of it all either. He would bring to mind scriptures such as, *"Of such a one will I glory: yet of myself I will not glory, but in mine infirmities,"* from 2 Corinthians 12:5.

Another scripture he gave me was from 1 Corinthians 10:13 that says, *"There hath no temptation taken you but such as is common to man; but God is faithful, who will not suffer you to be tempted above that ye are able; but will with the temptation also make a way to escape, that ye may be able to bear it."*

I knew God was with me, but I pondered why deliverance was not manifesting. Finally, at a Sunday night service God gave me understanding. God, not

Satan or sin, was allowing my distresses. God was turning up the heat around me spiritually. He was doing this so I could be refined into the complete man He created me to be. The way of escape He provided for me to remain in the fire but survive and grow by living and walking in it.

The content of scripture is so many times underestimated because the words do not seem real like our life's experiences. Just because someone underestimates the life in the Word of God, does not make its power of no effect. However, they will not experience its power fully in their everyday lives.

"Wherein ye greatly rejoice, though now for a season, if need be, ye are in heaviness through manifold temptations: that the trial of your faith, being much more precious than of gold that might perisheth, though it be tried by fire, might be found unto praise

and honor and glory of the appearing of Jesus Christ."
(1 Peter 1:6-7)

Yes, oftentimes we reap punishment for sowing seeds not of a righteous kind. Also know that the refining fire of God is for our growth. It is needed to at times carry us into a greater appreciation and understanding of God. God's love and mercy are never so welcomed as when a fire has burned a Christian down to his or her purest form. No matter how many acts of faith, habits of lack of prayer and a lack of reading your Bible will begin to disturb you. Let the fire of God begin to reveal more of what made you. Let your ungodly thoughts begin to disgust you. Let your faith be in God (besides being saved from hell) He will satisfy you. You will not only cry out to God, but you will embrace Him refining you in these and other matters very quickly.

There was a man who in the physical plane experienced the refining fire of God. Jacob, when he was at one of his most vulnerable times of his life, was thrown into a physical refining fire.

The Bible does not go into great lengths to describe Jacob's emotional, physical, or spiritual duress. It merely says Jacob was afraid, distressed, and lonely. At times we have all been left alone with our thoughts and perhaps even physically for a time which may have caused us to question who really cared about us. Now, these words seem to imply trouble, but do not really tell the whole story.

Imagine yourself having just escaped a life-threatening situation and traveling with all you have, family and possessions. Then you receive news your brother is on the way with 400 armed men. This happens to be the same brother whose last words were that he would kill you for your trickery and robbery that you had done to him.

Distressed! Afraid! Alone! Do these words describe all you would feel? Trial, test, and temptation might fit the bill as well.

Christians often quote it but living through and in trials, tests, and temptation can bring about a wealth of spiritual gifts that cannot accurately be stated.

Jacob, at the lowest time in his life, was met by a shadowy man- a man who the Bible does not even introduce by name. The Bible gives no genealogy, physical characteristics, or origin of him. We are suddenly taken from a physical description of where Jacob is alone to a description of a wrestling mat.

Doesn't God do this to us? God will have set us up through some circumstances that seem impossible to overcome alone to take us to another level in our Christian walk (see Genesis 32:22-30).

Just as the man did not prevail against Jacob, the fire is not sent to prevail over us. It merely serves to bless us through the trial. If you have ever lifted weights, you know the godly principle displayed in this story and Christians' lives. You place more weight on the barbell to increase your strength. God turns up the refining fire because He wants to increase your strength.

Yes, God could do it in a simpler fashion, but He said in His Word that fire is the way we are refined. We are God's creation and the quicker we are to seek how to be in His Will and stop trying to get Him to conform to ours, the better off we will be. God is always working a good work. Seeing that this is the case, let God use and work in you.

People want to know God's will. Christians need to be asking *to be in* God's will. God's work is not diminished or halted because I do not understand all God has for me to do (see Acts 8:26-40).

Realize that being led by the Spirit is just that, being led. Sometimes the path is clear. Promises and help abound along the way. In some cases, we can only see enough to take one step at a time and listen to our Father's still small voice say, "This is the way."

God's Word says that if any man lacks wisdom, let him ask God who will give it to him liberally. This is not an invitation to seek to read God's mind. This is an invitation to be wise enough to know how to follow God's leading. When you do not know for sure if it is God, ask Him for wisdom to know. Wait until you know before you move.

II. Flags.

"She laid it in the flags." (Exodus 2:3)

Throughout walking in fires that God allows us to go through, some circumstances and experiences standout in our memories. For me, it was when my former fiancée and I felt betrayed by one another. For King David, his affair with Bathsheba had to stand out. But as the Bible attests to you and I: God will bring us through. He will not only bring us through, but we will shine as gold or silver does once the impurities have been removed.

Throughout this process faith is the key. Christians must realize that the faith that God gives us must be used in everyday life. The Bible says faith without works is dead. Works does not always mean physical involvement by you.

The flags in the context of Exodus 2:3 refers to weeds or plants.

"And when she could no longer hide him, she took for him an ark of bulrushes, and daubed it with slime and with pitch, and put the child therein; and she laid it in the flags by the river's brink." (Exodus 2:3)

For the sake of spiritual understanding, I am using the word flag to describe a spiritual revelation or an uncovering or revealing of something by the Holy Spirit. This is just not a bright idea or a figment of my mind, but a revelation from the Lord.

Spiritual flags are circumstances that are engineered by God that can only be successfully navigated by an act of unusual faith. Unusual not because it is a different kind of faith, but unusual because the faith led to an extraordinary action on the part of the individual. These difficult circumstances were not the result of sin but the will of God so He could be glorified by the victory achieved.

The first flag God led me to is Pharaoh ordering the two midwives of the Hebrews to kill all of the baby boys born to the Hebrews (see Exodus 15:17). God gave these women boldness not to do this. About this time, a son is born to a man and woman of Levi. The woman found the child godly and so hid him for three months (see Exodus 2:1-2). The act of unusual faith was that after three months of risking death by hiding this child, the mother made a basket, placed the child inside it, and laid it by the river's brink.

Stop and think. What woman in the same situation would have stopped hiding the child only to place him in a basket where anyone could find him? Or any animal could kill him? What was this mother thinking?

Perhaps like her ancient relative, Abraham, she knew God was able to keep him alive or even raise him from the dead if he did die (see Hebrews 1:19).

Yes, the mother did have the child's sister watching the basket, but from a far distance. This act of physical faith of making a basket and placing the baby inside and then trusting God to work a miracle yielded a plethora of blessings to the Hebrew people.

There will be flags in your life. Know that when God first blessed you in the area where uncertainty is now, He had a plan. You did not receive the miracle by knowing how it all came about. You received the blessing because you knew God and served Him.

This child in this chapter of Exodus became known as Moses and during his childhood he was raised by his natural mother in a wealth and safety many of his fellow people never knew (see Exodus 2:10). He was known as the son of Pharaohs' daughter.

Physical worms with faith overcame this flag. Belief and trusting God was not enough without it. Sometimes you can only do the next thing God leads you to do. You do not know what the result will be, but you know God is in it. God has and will use your specific acts of faith for good.

The second flag God took me to is in Samuel. The circumstances were that a woman named Hannah was barren because the Lord had shut her womb (see 1 Samuel 1). The act of unusual faith on Hannah's part was to pray a sincere prayer to God out of her heart. This was an act of unusual faith in that it was customary to give one's servant to one's husband, and the children brought forth were considered the husband's wife's children. Another custom also practiced was to pray to idols or seek help from witches to have children. Hannah did neither of these, instead she prayed fervently to who she knew as the one true God. The result was she became pregnant and gave birth to Samuel the prophet.

This flag was overcome by a spiritual act of faith. The prayer, and only the prayer, moved the flag out of the way. You too, speaking to your heavenly father from a sincere heart, can get things done in your life.

Samuel went on to do great things for God, such as anoint Israel's first king and lead God's people until the time of the next king. Spiritual faith to pray overcame this flag. Others wanting and praying for her was not enough.

Finally, the third flag God led me to is in chapter two of Joshua. The circumstances of this flag were that spies had been sent to the City of Jericho. Upon entering the city, they went to lodge at the house of a harlot named Rahab. The spies were seen going into Rahab's house and it was reported to the king. The king then proceeded to send word to Rahab to bring the men to him.

Most would say the spies' mission was a flag. This would seem a good choice because we have a set of circumstances where a bad report of the spies could have cost Israel entering the land as it did before in Numbers 13 and 14. There is also the fact that two righteous men entered a harlot's house. This was not normal. An inn would have been more secretive because an innkeeper is used to strangers. A harlot was usually known to everyone and would typically sell information for a price.

But take note...the spies are not the flag. The harlot, Rahab, is. You have a woman who has only heard about the one true God of Israel but feared Him and made up her mind that given the chance she would serve Him. How do I know? Read Joshua 2:9-13.

This woman took her life in her hands to hide these spies and send the king a false report. She also asked the spies to save her and her family and all they had. The act of unusual faith on this woman's part was she that heard of the Lord, feared Him, and trusted in Him enough to make a request for not only her, but her family. As you see the story unfold, God not only delivered Rahab from destruction, but also her family and all they had. Can't you see it? Mighty warriors bargaining with a harlot based on what God would do.

"But Joshua had said unto the two men that had spied out the country, Go into the harlot's house, and bring out thence the woman, and all that she hath, as ye swore unto her." (Joshua 6:22)

Fearing God would have only saved Rahab's life, but she feared, believed, *and* asked. Fear of God to change her circumstances and believing in His abundant power is what overcame this flag.

Hearing about what God can do in your life is not enough for it to be done for you. You must hear, put confidence in what you have heard, and ask for what you want.

In these times of poverty and violence, you must believe that by sending our children to church, reading the Bible with them, and following God's commands, God will make a way despite obstacles. You must believe that by your physical actions of faith, God will deliver our children from whatever and then bless them.

We must realize that prayers and fasting do what arms and legs cannot. Even if the problem is physical, a spiritual battle fought and won with God's help can bring a manifestation of physical victories and blessings.

As you identify your flags, remember the making of the basket, the effectual prayer, and fearing God enough to obey and make requests of Him. The prophet Jeremiah said, *"But his word was in mine heart as a burning fire shut up in my bones, and I was weary with forbearing, and could not stay,"* (Jeremiah 20:9).

How would you feel if your child smoked drugs, but you never told them the dangers or sin in it and then they died? How would you feel if God blessed you to teach a person to read, but you never read the Bible? Then one day they asked you if you believed in God, and if so, why you never read the Bible to them. How would you feel if you worked with someone for years, but never told them about Jesus? Then one-day tragedy struck in their life. Then you prayed for them, and they asked you why you had not told them about your beliefs before now.

These feelings that you would likely have in response to these situations are the same as Jeremiah's forbearing of the fire shut up in his bones.

He had faced insults, experienced disappointments, and wanted never to speak for God again.

With wisdom and experience, emptiness, anticipation, and visions swirling in his mind, he felt a fire. This was a fire whose source would not let him give up. This fire that would not be put out by worries of what others thought, insecurities he felt about himself, or by confusion concerning how God would work it all out.

Some reading this book know that a fire should be there, but only faint warmth exists. There is warmth. There is a flicker. But due to lack of use and honesty within oneself, the flicker has not grown into a flame.

It only takes a spark to get the fire growing. The fire that each of us needs inside of us every day is the Word of God. It is bread to the poor in spirit, fire embers of life, understanding, and wisdom to the individual who gives their life to God.

This day, pray to God for a made-up mind for your thoughts to burn with the fire of God's Word. Be one who ignites others to greater service to God. Be wildfire for the Lord whose effects consume luke warmness, false doctrines, and sins of this world. Walk in the fire of saints. You are needed to light the way for others, spark the flames of dedication in others, and be a living, ever-burning fire of life to outshine the dead of this world and be outshone by the brightness of Christ. Never run from the fire. Always seek to be the fire that Satan runs from, and the children of God run to.

Chapter 11
"He Must Needs
Go Through Samaria"

"And he must needs go through Samaria."
(John 4:4)

At first glance, this scripture seems to only infer

an area or location Jesus had to travel through. This is

a plenary truth, a truth that becomes more detailed and

fuller over time. You must allow the Holy Spirit to

minister the meaning as well as the lesson behind these few words.

First, we must find out what Samaria was considered in Jesus' day. We then must realize what the equivalent of Samaria is spiritually to us.

Why spiritually? Because as I inferred earlier, there is meaning behind the text that is only understood and taught by the Holy Spirit. I know this disagrees with the world's reading comprehension rules. The fact is that anyone who tries to read the Bible from only an intellectual point of view will not fully grasp the revelation or understanding God intends. Though the Bible is written, it also is spirit.

In Jesus' time, Samaria was an area populated by a "mixed race" of Jewish people. The people had their roots originally from Jews, but through intermarriage with non-Jews they became a mixed (blood) race. In Jesus' time the two facts that really separate the people of Samaria and Jews (the latter being Jesus' lineage) were the mixed blood of the Samaritans and the fact that the Samaritans claimed Shechem rather than Zion the true Bethel (House of God).

You must grasp the fact that the history of the Samaritans and Jews was one of hate, segregation, and strong rivalry. You must also realize that these people had some of the same ancestors, beliefs, and hopes. This truly set the stage for turmoil, miscommunication, and jealousy.

In chapter four of Ezra, the Samaritans are trying to be part of building God's temple, but they were spurned and told they should have no part of its building. This and other confrontations set the stage of intolerance between the Samaritans and Jews in Jesus' time.

When the statement is made that, *"He must needs go through Samaria,"* we should acknowledge the gravity of it. Here was a man riding on the wave of God's favor and glory saying he had to go through His people's (the Jews) enemy's land. There is more than meets the eye here, and enemies and friends knew this.

Jesus could have gone around Samaria to get to Galilee; but he did not. Jesus' need to go through Samaria was not a geographical one. It was not a political or social need. The truth be told, it was for one lost soul (see Matthew 18:10-14).

Look at the scriptures after Jesus arrived in Samaria to see this truth.

"Then cometh he to a city of Samaria which is called Sychar, near the parcel of ground that Jacob gave to his son Joseph. Now Jacob's well was there.

Jesus therefore, being wearied with his journey, sat thus on the well: and it was about the sixth hour. There cometh a woman of Samaria to draw water: Jesus saith unto her Give me to drink. (For his disciples were gone away unto the city to buy meat). Then saith the woman of Samaria unto him, How is it that thou, being a Jew, askest drink of me, which am a woman of Samaria? for the Jews have no dealings with the Samaritans." (John 4:5-9)

Then, Jesus goes on to witness to the woman about the life which is found in Him. The woman asks for this life ("Give me this water," v.15). She then proceeds to be a witness for and about Jesus and is the vessel which God planted seeds of life in Samaria.

Now read John 1:10-30 for me to properly impart the fully applicable-to-life meaning of John 4:5 9 to you.

I must verse by verse give you the understanding God gave me.

"Then cometh he to a city of Samaria, which is called Sychar." (John 4:5)

Jesus never entered the city. Though he came to the outer limits of the city, he never entered.

Daily, we as Christians must in same shape or form be against sin. We do not have to partake in it, but because this world is sinful, we are around it. Remember that no matter what your circumstances or society, you can be kept by God. From the political conformity of Washington's upper class to the gang-infested neighborhoods of -south Chicago, to the unbelief that exists in churches throughout suburbia America: God can use, keep, and love you.

Jesus' mission required his presence in an area of Samaria. The love of God in you requires you to reach physically out to those around you who need Christ. Do not ever assume that because God sent you to an area you must jump headfirst into its most difficult areas. Jesus didn't. He allowed God to place him where God knew he would be a drop of hope, preceding the rainstorm of salvation.

Be that drop. Be what God enables and sends you to be, not what your good intentions and human reasoning say you ought to be. Walk comfortably in faith whenever God sends you. He has gone before you and has been at work before you ever arrived. God does not send you somewhere to fail. Just know the results are not about what you expected, but what God intended. Christians who do not keep this in mind often don't appreciate how God is using them.

"Jesus therefore, being wearied with his journey, sat thus it on the well: and was about the sixth hour." (John 4:6)

Jesus' physical weariness from his journey caused him to be right where God wanted him. Young man or woman, elder man or woman, middle-aged man, or woman, realize that your physical burnout and weighty problems are sometimes the avenue God uses to have you help someone else make it to Him. Your physical exhaustion may place you in the path of someone spiritually dead.

Stop focusing on exercise programs, sleep methods, and other forms of motivation. Ask God to open your understanding and show you why at times you are wearied. Ask God to show you why you cannot study or prepare for a sermon at the time you want.

So often people look at a problem only from their own personal problematic point of view. Personal inconveniences can be revelations God has for you. Ask God to show you how Heaven is viewing your circumstances of weariness (see James 1:5). God is not hampered by the limits we are.

If God is the priority in your life, remember He is the same all of the time.

For those that are unsaved, know that your circumstances are for the purpose of bringing you to God. He created the human body. God gave us the capacity to be weary for a reason. Just as everyone is unique, so are the functions and capacity of everyone. Stop trying to live up to this world's standards and instead ask God to help you live up to His will for you. When you do, you will go forth and be blessed in knowing that God truly understands and wants to help you.

"There cometh a woman of Samaria to draw water. Jesus saith unto her, Give me to drink." (John 4:7)

Jesus was now able to help, through his witness, a woman that God wanted to be a part of His family. Christian, you must begin to exercise the vocal aspect and Godly wisdom of your profession to effectively minister Christ to others. You must ask people questions, listen to their and God's answers, and then vocalize the answer God tells you. To truly be a good witness for Christ you must ask God to help you take advantage of opportunities He gives you to help others.

As children we picked up on our parents' expectations for our behavior and fed into them to get what we wanted. Now, we as Christians must seek Gods' face to learn what others around us need. We must not only recognize the needs but meet them as the Holy Spirit leads us. Be bold for Christ. People's eternal lives are dependent upon it (see Luke 9:26).

"For his disciples were gone away unto the city to buy meat." (John 4:8)

Though Jesus did not enter the city, his disciples did. Just because others go here or there does not mean you should. You do not need to go places just because everyone else is going. Your steps are ordered by the Lord. His purpose may not always be clear, but just obey His voice and trust Him.

How many souls have been lost because people would attend a church because of tradition rather than unction? Your peers may lead you to church, but only Jesus can lead you to Heaven. Never be pressured about how you should serve God. If everyone was in church every time the doors opened, there would be no prison ministries, street ministries, evangelism, or missionaries.

I am not saying to go to church. I am saying seek God's will for you, not only in every church service, but every aspect of your life. Christians worry about where other Christians are, more than they concern themselves about who is not even a Christian yet.

Anything not done in faith is a sin. Nothing is a given but God's goodness and love. Daily seek God to find out His agenda for you. There is someone at that park, mall, or job who needs you. Ask God! He will lead you to the place to where He can use you to help others. How many times have you, without thinking, found yourself in a place and position to help someone? Now consider how many places could you be to help someone with God directing you (see Galatians 5:16-18)?

"Then saith the woman of Samaria unto him, How is it that thou, being a Jew, askest drink of me, which am a woman of Samaria? for the Jews have no dealings with the Samaritans." (John 4:9)

The woman could not understand why Jesus would ask her to give him anything. The world does not and cannot understand the love of God or why God wants them to come to know Him. You and I are only blessed to know the answers to these questions because of God's gifts of salvation and His Word (the Bible). Christians must stop being so amazed and affronted by the fact that unsaved people may think there are ulterior motives or selfish gains behind Christianity (see 1 Corinthians 2:9-16). We must stop expecting all to embrace Jesus Christ as Lord and Savior without questions and unbelief. Once we realize

God must draw people to Him and it is God in us, we will walk in peace (not pressure) in doing God' s work.

Hopefully, you now better understand how Jesus' trip to Samaria is a foreshadowing of our daily trips through Samaria. It is not merely a physical place Jesus traveled to in order to save a soul, but Samaria is a place that has symbolism in our daily lives. It is a place that is foreign to us in taste, culture, and beliefs but familiar to us in beginnings, experiences, and hopes.

There is a good example of this symbolic Samaria in the Bible. When David was on the run from Saul, he found himself cast into the role of a rebellious subject of the king. David was forced to hide throughout Philistine territories. He truly could trust only God while in these lands.

But David had been in hard situations before, for David was once a shepherd boy. He had lived in the pastures and had only God to trust and believe in. David fought off enemies of the sheep while alone just as while on the run he fought off enemies of Israel (God's sheep) (see I Samuel chapters 20-30).

I bring this revelation to life because there are people reading this book who wonder how they can minister where God is leading them when they have no background in this area. I tell you that it is in the same way a shepherd boy (David) was instilled with the attributes of a king in the fields of his father's sheep. I want you to understand that.

Wherever God has you in life and whatever experiences you have had up to this point have readied you to fulfill your witness in Samaria. Do not be intimidated by your lack of a troubled background if God says go to prisons and help build my kingdom. Do not be intimidated by your lack of notoriety if God says speak in public forums and before large crowds and help build my kingdom.

God can use anyone to do anything. He used a man who was incarcerated to deliver some revelations, hope, and wisdom that He knew you needed to hear...ME!

You need not fear. You understand, minister, and make a difference to others for God. It is not you but God that chooses to use you in all these things. Throughout the Bible, men and women equipped by God were used to build God's kingdom and tear down Satan's.

Today, everything in life from dominoes to sports to work to school, etc. are opportunities for you to learn spiritual truths to apply throughout life. Samaria is daily traveled through. To the saved it is a chance to be used by God to give life. To the unsaved it is merely a place to hear about and accept life.

Chapter 12
Conclusion

I praise God for allowing me to be used to share His wisdom.

When I began this book, I was excited about the visions and revelations God gave me to share. I experienced every chapter of this book. I know that if it had not been for my incarceration, I would not have had the inspiration, time, or passion to write this book.

As I journeyed back through this book, my faith in God was strengthened even more. Just to see the daily relevancy of how God's Word comes together to help God's people in everyday life. Wow! I pray this book and the lessons within find you at home, work, the gym, the plane, or wherever you may go (see Joshua 1:9).

Be blessed and keep studying God's Word to show yourself an approved worker of God. Thank you for taking the time to read this book. I pray that the truths in it draw you closer to God and closer to His people.

Sean

About the Author

Sean Oliver is a proven leader, trusted mentor, and strong Christian business advisor. During incarceration, Sean found God and his true-life purpose. With years locked away in maximum security units, he had significant time to evaluate the decisions that landed him in prison. His peers grew to count on his advice, as one who could provide a word of strong encouragement, but who could also be trusted to deliver a tough message of change. His life was dedicated, not merely to serving out his term, but to investing his time in others, and through that process, becoming the best version of himself that he could be. Freedom has provided new opportunities for Sean to continue his mission to help others. He works as a Community Coordinator for Life Anew, an organization that uses restorative justice as a means of fostering culture and climate in communities all around the world. Sean also founded Open Doors Consulting which equips others with better decision-making tools. He shares God's Word of hope in his biblical teachings on radio, social media platforms, including Facebook, Instagram, Tik Tok, and his YouTube channel *Open Doors to Better Relationships*.

To learn more about Sean visit www.opendoorstobetter.com

Courses Sean created:

Probation Course: Making Better Decisions

Digital Court Diversion Decision Making Course: **STOP**

Rehabilitation/Reentry Curriculum for Returning Citizens to help navigate life after incarceration: **TAKE TWO**

*Speaking Topics Sean presents: ***Finding My Significance, Making Better Decisions, Post Incarceration Syndrome***

Made in the USA
Columbia, SC
17 February 2023

12566235R00187